About the author

As a young man, Vernon Kitabu Turner discovered poetry for self-expression and martial arts for self-defense. His initiation by Zen master Nomura-Roshi in 1967 changed his writing, and made him a true Bushido warrior.

Throughout his life, he has continued to develop his writing as an author, journalist and a poet. He was initiated by Zen master Nomura Roshi in 1967, and recognized as a spiritual teacher by Master Sant Keshavadas of the Vishwah Ashanti Temple, and has been called 'one of the most prominent voices of our time' in the international anthology *The Way Ahead*, which features his work along with that of the Dalai Lama and Nobel Laureate Vaclav Havel.

By the Same Author

Kung Fu: The Master

The Secret of Freedom

Soul to Soul

Soul Sword

under the sword

Life Lessons to Awaken the Zen Warrior in you

VERNON KITABU TURNER

WATKINS PUBLISHING
LONDON

This edition first published in the UK and USA 2012 by
Watkins Publishing, Sixth Floor, Castle House,
75–76 Wells Street, London W1T 3QH

Design and typography copyright © Watkins Publishing 2012
Text Copyright © Vernon Kitabu Turner 2012

Vernon Kitabu Turner has asserted his right under the Copyright,
Designs and Patents Act 1988 to be identified as the author
of this work.

1 3 5 7 9 10 8 6 4 2

Designed and typeset by Jerry Goldie Graphic Design

Printed and bound by Imago in China

British Library Cataloguing-in-Publication Data Available

Library of Congress Cataloging-in-Publication Data Available

ISBN: 978-1-78028-098-1

www.watkinspublishing.co.uk

Distributed in the USA and Canada by Sterling Publishing Co., Inc.
387 Park Avenue South, New York, NY 10016-8810

For information about custom editions, special sales, premium and
corporate purchases, please contact Sterling Special Sales
Department at 800-805-5489 or specialsales@sterlingpub.com

CONTENTS

INTRODUCTION

In one way or another, we are all being tested. Every day of our lives.

Sometimes, the matter is simple and non-threatening. We may be trapped in a long line when we are short on time. How do we handle that moment? Do we become irritable, impatient? That is a test.

How we handle so common a problem as this could easily determine the outcome of more serious matters. Learning to cope with the little things can preserve our wellbeing or even save our life, or that of a loved one.

A game is a contest between two or more forces. It does not matter if one's opponent is a machine, an object. What matters is that an activity is initiated by someone or something outside of our own field of control – such an action requires our response. How we respond determines whether we have 'won' or 'lost' the encounter.

If we are playing a computer game, the win/lose factor may be entirely psychological. Nothing is really gained or lost in that situation. A problem comes up when there is the possibility of genuine loss, whether that loss be measured financially, emotionally or in physical trauma.

Years ago the American game company Milton Bradley

sold a boardgame called *The Game of Life*. The theme followed the player down the road of life from business ventures to building a family, to a possible end of wealth or poverty. When I played it as a teenager I found the details so realistic and my drive to win so strong that, on those occasions when I landed in the poorhouse, I felt that it was really true. I did not want that outcome.

If the gamer paid attention to the messages of play, it could be seen that an important lesson was being taught: *focus on how you spend your money; make good decisions or pay the price.* The game also had its measure of luck. We moved along the 'path of life' based on the toss of the die … and so it is in real life. We never know what is in store for us from one moment to the next. We can only plan for the expected, but that does not mean we are helpless when faced with the unexpected. We can take out a board game whenever we want. We can log into a video game whenever we have a box or connection, but the biggest game of all is always on, and we do not always get to choose what we will play.

The game of life goes on within the box (in homes and buildings of all kinds) and in the world-at-large. It can be enjoyable, a stimulating experience, or it can be nerve-wracking or dangerous. We never know. What is certain is the unpredictability of the game. Thus, in that sense, life is an X-Game, a game of unknown quantities.

When aliens or monsters leap at you from a computer screen you have a moment to react, but most likely you are fully aware that there is no real danger to your person. There will be no bodily harm if you fail. You are braced, hunched over, almost belted into your seat as you focus on dispatching the attackers. In the video game you are safely outside the box where danger abounds.

The real world is a different story. You may still be outside the box, but so is everything that is coming your way. It's time to take off the seat belt and stand at the ready. Everyday life is always a war-game in one way or another. If we strive to be safe and advance in this world, we need to keep before us the idea that we are under the sword.

> An ancient teacher once said
> to a frightened warrior
> reluctant to face death by cold steel,
> 'Under the sword held high
> is hell making you tremble ...
> But go on anyway, go forth,
> without looking back,
> without harboring a single thought of tomorrow
> or the next moment.'
> Then, right there,
> right there as you move forward,
> wielding your own sword,
> an irresistible force ...
> right then,
> you will experience Heaven.

We worship the outcome of things and, by so doing, we miss the virtue in the process – the steps, the journey itself. There is no guarantee of the future arriving, but here we are, now, doing this. Do this fully with all of your being. Right here, this moment is Heaven. Gamers of all types develop exclusive focus – everything else around them seems to vanish. There is only the game. This is a form of *samadhi*, the concentration power that is a prerequisite to enlightenment.

However, this game focus is not enough. We must learn how to take our specialized skills and adapt them to the real world. That is where the Game of Life and its battles are played for the highest stakes of all. There will be challenges. The adversary will raise his sword high and the keenness of his blade may make you weak with fear. Remember the ancient teacher: *focus and charge ahead*. There is nothing to turn back to.

CHAPTER ONE

THE GAMER, THE ZEN WARRIOR

As very young children we opened our eyes to a world where everything was fresh and exciting. It did not matter how others looked upon what we saw. Dirt was fascinating to play with. All around us were colors, motion and sounds. We looked without seeing. We listened without hearing and we experienced without understanding. Our natural responses were simple. All things solicited a gurgle, a smile or a cry. With these few tools we received and communicated with those who peopled our environment.

In the ideal situation everything comes to the child, just as water and nourishment flow of their own accord to the tree, planted unmoving in the field. The Great Divine takes care of the plants and animals, but our parents are entrusted with our lives … and in that ideal environment, made ideal by the care of the parents, the child is provided for to the best of their abilities. If a house is filled with love it will not matter whether it is a mansion on a hill or public housing on Poor Street. The sense of wellbeing for little ones comes from a loving hug, from genuine concern or a gentle spirit. When a child feels loved and appreciated, it feels safe. The child can rest.

Rest does not meant reclining. No, this rest is a spiritual sense that frees the mind of the child to focus on the activities at hand. When a child is at rest spiritually, he or she has no need to look back. Looking back is the first sign of uncertainty, the first mistake a Gamer or Zen Warrior can make. It is a giant misstep that will lead to other problems as we move down the road in the Game of Life. *So don't look back!*

The child who would walk must first stand. The little one usually leans on a chair or a parent when he or she takes those first tentative steps away from support. Some children are pushed out into the 'void'. When they lose their balance, they may expect a helping hand. When it doesn't come, they cry pitifully. Some parents will pick up their child and comfort it, and others will not. The child may continue crying until exhausted. This child may feel betrayed by those who urged him on, uncertain about what happened. Children expect someone to run to their aid at every turn.

There are some children who, having been watchful of those around them, venture out all alone into the 'void', the space empty of support. They fall to the floor, realize they are not hurt and rise to try again. These children may laugh at their efforts, even at the falling. They rise and fall and keep reaching toward the far distance. They never look back.

There are so many adventures ahead. You may not think of walking as such a huge accomplishment, but it was when you did it the first time. It takes drive and courage for the war veteran who has lost a limb or for the victim of a debilitating disease to rise above disfigurement and weakness to step out into the playing field again, but it can be done if you don't look back.

You are sitting at a game console engaged in an online battle. What would happen if you were also watching an exciting movie at the same time? Every time the music swelled, you would look back to see what was happening on the screen. By the time you refocused on the 'battlefield' you would be disoriented for a moment. You would need to synch with the timing of the game again – thank God it is only a game. The distraction will cost you a few points, or a pretend life, at worst.

Looking back and forth indicates a divided mind. This is a major flaw in the use of the mind. The more we encourage such behavior, the more likely we are to rob ourselves of *prajna paramita*, that instinctive wisdom demonstrable through action. Hesitation is death: the vacillating mind triggers many problems.

It has not been overlooked by great thinkers and spiritual emissaries through the ages. Where there is fear there will no doubt be hesitation, vacillation and stopping of the mind. Problems also arise from a lack of concentration or commitment to the activity at hand. It is no wonder that the Lord admonishes the believer never to turn back even once, when putting his hands to the plow, or that Lot is told to leave Sodom and Gomorrah, doomed cities both, without looking back upon the destruction.

The Zen master also instructs the disciple to go forth without looking back … *mo chi chu*. This is not an easy thing to do. We consider caution to involve moving along in a gingerly way, but what happens when we introduce the element of time? The shorter the time allowed, the less time there is to reflect upon action. The lack of time can produce tension. With tension comes nervousness. One's discipline and precision can vanish in a moment. What do we do then?

The cart won't go. What do you hit? The cart or the horse? Well, you could beat the cart for a while.

In life we face many unknowns. Every day brings the unexpected, though most unknowns escape our awareness. A measure of physical health is something to be grateful for, yet dexterity of the mind is something to be treasured far more. When we have a mind that is adaptable, we can play the game before us. This presence of mind inspires the fingers to fly in accord with what the eyes see. A game is just a window on an imaginary world. We want to extend our awareness and respond to the larger world. In the real world, we may find ourselves under the sword at any time and in many different ways.

We must prepare for the unknown right now. We must be willing to play the X-Game.

By X-Game I do not mean a particular brand of game or sport but a type of play in which the variables are not easily identifiable at once. There are surprises. The Gamer/Warrior must be alert to the sudden shifts and rapid activities on the screen. Seeing is not enough – his hands must be able to act in accord with his eyes to push the right buttons, grab the right level or otherwise interact with the images before him.

American baseball is like this. The players know that a ball is going to come, but the batter does not know what pitch will be thrown, nor how high or how low it will come. The opposing players know that the ball may be hit into the field, but they do not know where it will go. For the batter his focus must be restricted to a limited area, while those whose duty it is to catch the struck ball must keep a broader state of awareness. It is a given that all of the players can run, jump, catch and throw to various degrees, but these abilities must come together seamlessly to produce a true athlete and a successful play.

To excel at anything, to take decisive action, always requires a measure of faith. A racecar driver must have faith in his driving ability to race down the track at high speeds but he must also trust his pit crew and the car he is driving. How strong a contender would he be if he believed his brakes or steering were to fail when he needed them most? If this idea was firmly planted in his thoughts, no other driver would have to outmaneuver him – he would simply lose the race by his own diminished effort.

If we play chess recklessly without observing the board we will hear 'Checkmate!' embarrassingly soon. *Something is coming our way.* We do not know what. In an actual game, even the tension can be counted as fun. But in the larger Game of Life, what we face may be anything but fun. We have to prepare ourselves.

It is my prayer that each of you lives a long, healthy and peaceful life. To do that, you cannot ignore that there are dangers in the world. Danger does not just befall the criminal, the violent and the poor. It can strike anyone. Some of the most beautiful and loving of people are victims of senseless attack.

As I write this, it is only three days since my favorite elementary school teacher was smothered to death in her own home. It was reported that someone pulled a plastic bag over the head of this wonderful 83-year old woman. As I felt the pain of this tragedy I also pondered on what could have been done, or what she could have done to preserve her life. Her loss helped me to see the importance of this book even more than before.

Given the right understanding, anyone, no matter how young or old, can act to preserve their wellbeing. We must first change the way we see our lives. The onboard computer, your brain, must be reprogrammed.

Let's take a closer look at the X-Factor. First of all, X stands for an active opposing energy that could very well be manifested as a person. A falling rock is energy but not a person. A pick-pocket is a person. The two conveyors of energy would not be handled in the same way. A Zen story may help to illustrate the way of a rock or another inert energy form.

> The Satori Beast was beautiful to look at. A woodcutter happened upon the mulch-colored floating creature while he was chopping wood. Secretly, he thought he would slay it to keep, as a trophy. When it was near him he swung his ax and missed widely. The creature dodged the attack easily. The woodcutter tried again but experienced the same result.
>
> The Satori started taunting him: 'You cannot catch me! I can read your mind.'
>
> Frustrated, the woodcutter gave up and just went back to simply chopping wood. At one point, in the midst of a mighty upward arc, the head of the ax flew off. When the woodcutter turned to see where it had flown he saw it resting on the body of the Satori. The creature could read the minds of men but it could not read the ax, which had no mind nor intention.

The story has a higher meaning, but it helps us to understand an important point. When facing the unknown we cannot always rely on known techniques and responses. To properly deal with X-factors in our life we must be able to come from X, the unconscious. We need to make No-Mind responses.

The left side of your body and the right side together make up one whole form. If one side is felled by disease, like a stroke, we would readily see that we are handicapped. Yet, in a far more subtle way, people ignore the range of abilities available to them when they are outside their comfort zone. The Gamer/Warrior must push past what is comfortable to unleash the possibilities of play and of real-life responses.

Long ago, when typewriters were considered an advanced tool, I learned to place my fingers on their home keys rather than peck along with one finger. As I became more familiar with the location of the keys I found I could type without looking. Sometimes my fingers would move across the keyboard with amazing speed. Then there would be a moment of doubt. My fingers would slow down and I would hit the wrong letter after streams of correct ones. What happened? The problem was not with my fingers but my mind. I blocked my flow by expecting a mistake.

So what do I hit? The cart or the horse? What will inspire me onward?

There are always things we can do to improve our game or our responses. That which we do have influence over, we should act upon. Body and mind are like balloons and air. Without air the balloon has no functionality. Without the balloon, air has no form. When the two parts come together they are both just the balloon. They become a toy to inspire joy and play.

Mind and body are like that. The mind is the air, the body is the balloon. Together they produce activity. If we are aware of the nature of the balloon we will avoid sharp objects when using it. If we are aware of the nature of the body, our own body, we are aware of our strengths and limitations and use it accordingly. That we understand our own body is vital to our success, as you will come to see.

No game can be played successfully if we misunderstand the basic rules of play. In chess, the knight, the bishop, pawns, king and queen each have their power. If we move them like checkers we will most certainly lose. But we can be clear about what a chess-piece can do.

We do not know how the opposing player will move. That is the X-factor. It does not matter whether we are playing chess, a video game or whether we're outdoors playing sports. There will always be an X-factor. How we deal with this may be the most important act of the game.

Here's a Zen Warrior lesson. Real life is not a game, but the elements of games can help us prepare for the unexpected in a relaxed and enjoyable way. All things are connected but we do not always recognize those connections. From this moment on, practice expanded awareness, and you will enjoy it.

No past mind, no future mind, no present mind – a Zen saying.

You may ask, 'If I have no past mind, no future mind and no present mind, wouldn't that leave me with no mind?' Yes, you would have No-Mind. Hearing or seeing the words may produce a negative or non-positive feeling, but the actual experience is dynamically alive. When we look back (to the past), forward (to the future) or try to find the now, we are short-circuiting the true mind. We are producing a projection of the real thing. No projection can be the real thing.

Now is the movement of your eyes across the page, the sounds in your environment, the location of the receiving instrument, your body. There is no other 'now' to be found. It is not a concept to grasp in some philosophical way. It is ice water on a sweltering day, your hands on the doorknob. Nothing will ever happen to you that does not take place in the present moment.

We have stated that this Game of Life, in play and for real, throws unknowns at us ... X-factors. People – perhaps you are one of them – tend to expect the familiar, the routine. In their walk or drive to school or work they do not see or hear the events on the road, or notice the scenery, as a rule, because they have traveled that path often. They see in a detached way and do not *look*. When we fail to look afresh we become deadened to our surroundings. We miss the life that is constantly being breathed into all things.

Not everything is about danger. On the road to the cemetery to say farewell to a beloved cousin, my sister and I admired the autumn leaves which emblazoned the trees along the highway. We had a lively discussion about their beauty. Under the circumstances, we could have overlooked Heaven's gift at that moment, but we were attuned enough to receive it as it made its illustrious appearance along the way. Awareness of the colorful leaves uplifted our spirits.

We will always notice the familiar. They are signs that tell us we are safe and at home. We are somewhere we have been before, or we are about to do something we have done so many times before. We move through this world on automatic. Automatic may be familiar, but it is not *alive*.

Years ago, long before my brother became a scholar, he told me he had found a job. 'What do you do?' I asked. 'I put numbers in a slot,' he said. 'So why do you put numbers in a slot?' 'I don't know. I just put the numbers in a slot.'

I never found out just why he did that, but I imagined that, after a while, he could slip numbers in the slot rapidly and without much thought. I wondered what would happen if he happened across an alphabet. That would be an unknown, an X-factor. Suddenly, his automatic and efficient method of working would break down. From the moment we open our eyes in bed we should expect the unexpected ... look for it ... be ready.

Don't look back

The road is straight, dark,
there is a single **point** of light.
It is the door
to where you want to be.
The howling wolf
runs behind you,
you feel the heat of its pursuit,
hear its massive paws
pounding the earth.
The road is straight, dark,
but don't look back.
There is a single point of light,
inviting you,
it is a place of refuge just waiting to receive you,
but don't look back.
Your mind is with what it sees.
What it meditates on, it becomes.
Stay focused on the light,
for soon it will be all that you see,
all that you are –
no more beast at your heels.
No more terrifying sounds.
Darkness flees when you guide your mind
to the single point of light.

CHAPTER TWO

HAND, EYE AND FOOT COORDINATION

We often hear the phrase, 'hand and eye coordination'. Athletes need that ability to perform their best. Workers in numerous occupations would find themselves in trouble on the job if their hands failed to work well with their eyes. Gamers keep their fingers at the ready to click, pull or push whatever tool is necessary to get their video avatars to act as they want them to act. With the advent of new gaming technology like Wii, people involve their whole bodies in response to the stimuli onscreen. On the one hand, this is fun. On the other, it can teach us valuable skills. We do not automatically transfer the skills acquired in a game to our daily life: for that to happen we must have a different mental attitude.

Even athletes may fail to respond wisely in an emergency. Fast eyes and hands are not enough. Fast feet are not enough to get us where we need to be when the unexpected occurs. Life is the only X-Game that we can lose forever. We need to cultivate a deeper appreciation for this precious treasure that we can lose at any moment.

Fortunately, there is a game plan, and you can train

anywhere to be a warrior. Most of us are born with every tool we will ever need to master the game. What is missing is proper instructions on how to coordinate them. There are countless teachings to put into practice. So you have hands and feet but, in a time when there is only a moment to react, will they remember how to run, jump or leap, or will you freeze? Missing a shot in a basketball game with friends may be annoying, but you will live. Failing to get out of the way of an out-of-control car could be fatal. The hands, eyes and feet of the Zen Warrior must work as one.

Here's another Zen Warrior lesson. *Just because our eyes are open, it does not mean we are seeing.* We need to take in our environment through our eyes and all of our senses as much as possible.

> Float like a butterfly,
> sting like a bee.
> Your hands can't hit
> what your eyes can't see.
> - *Muhammad Ali (then Cassius Clay)*

Zen Lesson: *seeing is awareness. Practice awareness.* If someone has moved something in the room, you should sense it. Take a moment to find out what is different.

When you swing your legs, preparing to place your feet on the floor, glance down to see where you are placing them. Sit on the edge of the bed a moment, take a deep breath, inhaling from the *tanden* (just below the naval), and raise your arms high above your head with your fingers outstretched. At the end of the exhalation, inhale with your arms still raised, then bring them down slowly with the next exhalation. Rest your hands upon your knees. Your back should be slightly arched backwards at the base of your spine. Now you are ready to move about the house. As you go from room to room, look and *see*, as if for the first time.

A Samurai warrior wanted to test the development of his sons in the Art of the Warrior. He placed a pillow above the door so that it would fall when someone entered. One by one he called his three sons. The youngest came first. The pillow fell as he entered. Drawing his sword, the boy struck the pillow with his sword as it hit the floor. The middle son entered. His sword flashed out and cut the pillow in two as it fell, midway.

When the oldest son arrived he stopped at the door before stepping through. Reaching up, he removed the pillow then walked into the room. The father was highly disappointed with his youngest son, and saw promise in the middle one. He was very pleased with the growth of the eldest. The two younger sons had responded to the challenge, but they did not accurately discern the nature of the problem. Both of them 'slew' the pillow. The eldest son sensed that something was different but his response was appropriate to the problem – after all, it was only a pillow. The eldest son practiced true seeing. Seeing is more than registering a picture. There must be understanding … wisdom connected to the act of seeing.

When I was a child I sat on a fence to watch a baseball game. At one point in the game I saw a white dot in the air. I blinked as it was instantly bigger. Suddenly I felt an impact to my head and everything went black. The dot was a baseball thrown wide by the pitcher. I saw it but I did not recognize what I was looking at. Had I known, I could have leaned out of the way of its trajectory. There was time. Instead, I saw only a white dot, not a hardball coming at me.

I fell from the fence to the ground, hurt by both the ball and the fall. People watching a ballgame do not expect to be struck by the ball, although there are many of them who hope they can catch a wayward pitch. A fan who dreams of catching such a ball is ready, hoping. This person is hyped up to leap and make contact, the moment the ball leaves the field. His eyes are focused ... tracking. This person is expecting the possible to happen.

Sadguru Sant Keshavadas, my teacher, told the story of a man who saw a huge snake as he was walking through the woods. He ran to the nearest tree and climbed it. For a long time he watched to see if the snake would move so that he could get down and continue his journey. The snake was still. Eventually, the man decided that the creature was dead. He came down from the tree and very carefully approached the resting place of the serpent. To his surprise, it was a rope.

'It is all right to superimpose the body of a snake on a rope,' Guruji said. 'But don't superimpose a rope on the body of a snake.' We laughed upon hearing that, but the message is very powerful. Are we seeing a friend instead of the snake who is pretending to be a friend? Look and see carefully.

Foyan, a 12th-century Zen master, taught that all appearances are unreal. 'The student of The Way must

learn that appearances are not inherent characteristics,'
he explains in the Thomas Cleary translation of his work,
Instant Zen. True *seeing* must go beyond appearance.
We cannot base our actions solely on what *appears to be*.
We should see as a mirror sees – accurately, instantly and
without interpretation. The images of the surrounding world
are reflected upon our consciousness without prejudice – the
blue of the sky, the green of the grass, the myriad colors
which meet us as we move through the day. We should
receive them all without stopping.

Zen Lesson: *go beyond the appearance of things*.

Awakening the Stallion

Have you forgotten that you are a stallion?
Remember how you galloped through the fields of
   your youth,
leaping, to land on your feet
with ease, without stress,
without worry?

Where are those legs and feet now? Have you
   forgotten them?
Have you ceased to glory in their power,
to expect more from them?
Are you afraid now to leap, to sprint?
Are you afraid even to stand?

Where has the stallion gone?
Is he still pawing the earth,
kicking against the stall,
eager to be free to run again?

Throw open the door.
Let your spirit run free again,
unbound by the number of years,
unlimited by the limited expectations of others.
You are, as it is written, what you think you
    are ...
'So as a man thinketh ...'

Free yourself, stand on sturdy feet, and run.
This time there is no destination,
there is just the running.
Feel the wind as you
race across the meadowland, right now.

CHAPTER THREE

THE POWER OF ONE HAND

Stretch out your hand for a moment. Move your fingers, make a fist. Now that is a beautiful and most remarkable piece of equipment, and it is sensitive also. It can appreciate the bark of a tree or the smooth skin of a baby. It can grasp a hammer or caress a loved one. It is wonderful, but do you really take any time out to give thanks, to pay homage to this tool that serves you so well? Now is that time. *Feel it*. Give it some love before we go one step further.

I have spoken of the hand, as a singular, for a reason. To go beyond the dualistic breakdown that keeps us indecisive and trapped, we need a way of fine-tuning ourselves. You have but one hand that is yours. Choose now which it shall be, the left or the right. If you chose the right (or the left), that will be your hand. This is the hand you will focus on and train. The other one is a shadow. It will act as a support, receiving its orders unconsciously. This is the faith you must put in it. This one hand of yours is connected. On the first level of understanding, it is connected to sight.

Which eye should you use, the left or the right? The answer is neither. Use the middle one, the Third Eye. There is no left or right there, so it is the One Eye.

When you think in terms of left or right, you focus on the outer or merely the physical appearance of what you are. That, as I have stated, is an incorrect view. Sadguru Sant Keshavadas taught that we human beings are not the body. To function at our best we must uncover the truth of our being. We need to function from the truth of our being, not out of delusion.

How do we cut duality in twain? Take one hand away. There will come a moment when even the one that is left will be taken away, but let us not go too far ahead. You have one hand. This sight you have, the power that recognizes sunsets and sunrises, does not depend on the physical eyeballs. In our practice, there is *seeing* without preoccupation with the instruments of sight. The substance of this One Eye is the hand, not just the hand but the body itself. It will respond to the seen like a dancer to music, once our transformation is complete.

Once I was sitting in the lounge of a famous hotel, the Waldorf Astoria. I was wearing a business suit that I reserved for those moments I needed to look successful. Not far away from me sat a thin little man sipping a cup of coffee. A few moments later I felt a touch. I looked over my shoulder to see the man squeezing the fabric of my suit. 'I am a tailor,' he said. 'I just wanted to see if this material was real.' The tailor needed to *see* – he got a clear picture with his hands. To him, reaching out and touching with his hand was no more intrusive than doing so with his eyes. They were one.

I was in a hotel lobby another time, but this time it was a seedy establishment in mid-Manhattan. I entered to hear a man cussing. He was dressed all in brown leather with a matching wide-brim hat. One hand clutched a pretty and provocatively dressed woman and the other was clenched in a fist. Immediately I yelled, commanding him not to hit her.

'This is my property,' he responded. 'I'll do what I want to her.'

'This is a public lobby,' I said. 'That makes it a public event.' He let her go and walked toward me. I stood my ground. When he was close to me, within touching distance, he whipped a knife out from under his coat. All I saw was a glint of light on steel, but in that instant my right hand intercepted his thrust and the knife was instantly in my hand. Almost before either of us could draw a breath, I aimed the blade between his legs and stopped short of penetrating his flesh. 'You are about to be out of business forever,' I said, the knife pressing against his 'major organ'.

Now that his attack was fully neutralized, all the aggression was gone. The pimp was helpless. I offered him a way out with dignity.

'Gentleman's agreement,' I said. 'Leave the lady alone and you can walk away.'

'I agree,' he said.

I stepped back and handed him his knife. 'Can you teach me that stuff?' he asked.

Among the people watching the drama had been the hotel security guards. They had remained silent the entire time but now they spoke up. They wanted me to teach them too.

In retrospect I ask myself, why did I return the knife? The pimp could have tried to cut me again. Still, it was his, so I gave it back. He kept his promise and yielded. What is more important is the *way* I took the knife. I did not know what was coming. I had no strategy. I was just watching the pimp approach me when suddenly he moved and revealed his blade. At the same time the knife sliced the air, my hand acted with its own mind and my body turned away from danger. His knife-hand was trapped too quickly for him to react. I seized the blade, but it was as if it magically appeared in my hand.

The incident took place in the 1970s at the Woodstock Hotel. A satori experience had not only transformed my perception of the world but awakened in me the spirit of self-defense. I stood before a threat with a mind empty of a preconceived plan. There was no trace of this understanding prior to taking this action, but afterwards whatever I did could be repeated or taught to others as a technique.

This was an act of faith. I had prayed for the wisdom and strength to defend myself and others. I had no idea how this ability would reveal itself. Facing the knife-wielding pimp was just one example of how effective defense can be when it arises unrestricted from the unconscious. I stepped forward and a miracle response arose. It was a classic No-Mind moment. I did nothing consciously, yet everything was done correctly. My hand acted of its own accord.

It may seem far-fetched to believe that you can gain the ability of a seasoned warrior without years of formal training and specialized conditioning. Well, formal training is one way to achieve your goal. If you go that route you will be taking a linear path that is centered on the body. Weight, height, strength and all the salient characteristics of success as a warrior are drawn from the material side of our existence. In this world, the bigger they are the harder they fall. There is another avenue. Forget the word Zen. Read instead, 'spiritual'.

If you learn to approach your study as a spiritual student you will see that the precedent for such transformations were established long ago. Consider Psalms 18:32-34 from the *Holy Bible*.

> 32. It is God that girdeth me with strength,
>   and maketh my way perfect.

> 33. He maketh *my feet like hinds' feet*, and
>   setteth me upon my high places.

> 34. He *teacheth my hands* to war, so that a
>   bow of steel is broken by mine arms.

The above verses reveal that the warrior-king David had incredible agility. He was fleet of foot and as agile as a deer (hind). We also see a reference to his hands as being taught the art of war. This verse speaks as if his hands had an independent life. Clearly, David's *sensei* (teacher) is the Lord – he is powered by God. To be powered by God requires a different kind of preparation than being trained by rote under human guidance. If you can make the proper shift in the way you use your mind, it leads to a shift in your performance as well. Enter this gate and time is compressed. To respond like a Zen Warrior in thirty days or less is easy. Making the proper shift in consciousness ... now that is what we must work on.

Your feet can perform like a hind's feet. You can run and leap. You can land safely. Now if you are getting up there in years, you may say such days are behind you, but never rule out what you can do in times of trouble. You may be surprised.

We will explore this theme a little before we leave this chapter. Take a moment to concentrate on your feet.

Consider all they do for you. When is the last time you thanked them or offered up thanks for them? Stop, this moment. Give thanks and direct some praise to your feet. If your limbs are prosthetic, be thankful that they exist to help you. How marvelous it is to have feet – tools that propel us through this world. *Feel* them. Do not stop sending them appreciation until something comes back.

Now that you have done that, plan to treat your feet to a pedicure, your hands to a manicure and pamper your eyes under a steamed towel and just let them relax. As you perform each of these procedures, single out the various parts of your body as the center of attention. It will not take long before you realize just how important each part is. Contemplate your feet as you move about. Recognize the support that they give.

As you do this, let your attention flow from their strong base to the twin flexible towers that are your legs. They, too, work as one – two legs, one motion. Each individual extension of the one knows what to do ... when you allow it. Using your left and right hand, massage your thighs in a downward and upward motion. Your eyes should be closed. Follow the sensations. Who is on the receiving end? The feeler of the sensations ... that person is you.

The *katana*, the beautiful Japanese sword treasured by the *Samurai* and all who appreciate works of art, was not just *made*. The creation of a single sword was brought about by the unity of substance, mind and spirit. The swordsmith was a master, a priest in his own right, who took time to bring forth the perfect sword. This priestly endeavor was directed at creating a marvelous instrument which would only come to life in the hands of a master. The master, like the sword, had undergone a unique process of cultivation.

In our case, the sword that is being prepared, the Soul Sword, is formed when Mind and Spirit work in unity to perform a single task. The sheath of that sword is not made of leather – it is your own flesh and blood. The sheath is fully visible but the sword is unseen. Sometimes, when under assault, a master will not reveal his blade – he keeps it in its sheath and moves the sheath as his weapon. No one sees the sword but it is in evidence by the sheer forcefulness of its covered strikes. Like that, your body can be moved about effectively. That which moves the sword moves the sheath. The master of the invisible *katana* is also master of the seen. The shadow follows the man, it does not lead him.

Your basic training has begun. You may be wondering how so simple a practice can awaken the warrior instinct in you. You may also be going, 'ahhh', remembering that 'Wax on, wax off' from the original *Karate Kid* movie, had purpose beyond the obvious.

> What do you hit if the cart won't go? The cart
> or the horse?
> Feel the sting of the lash? The Roshi is
> hitting you, horse.

We do not control the movements of others, but we can control our own. If we can master our own body to whatever extent possible, we can exert great influence over circumstances. It is time for you to change the way you look at your body and yourself. Your body is not the self, not yourself.

In the game world you sit at a console or computer where the controls are directed away from yourself. In this kingdom of you, the controls are directed within. You have potentially 360 degrees of awareness and more. Isn't that exciting? In a game, the movements of opposing forces are confined to the monitor or the game-board. In real life, adversarial forces may strike from any direction at any time. That is why seeing must not be tunnel-vision. We must *see* in the true sense, with the whole of our being. This is not the seeing of a tourist who does not want to miss any item of interest on a vacation. This is the seeing of a tiger, a seeing with the ears, the nostrils, the skin, not just the eyes.

Recently, one of my students returned from Brazil with wonderful stories of the sights he had seen. Unfortunately, one of the things he did not see was the thief who stole his laptop and suitcase while he stood in a nearby restaurant. He was not looking for that. In order to recognize potential danger, we have to acknowledge the possibility of trouble. If we do not accept the possibility, we overlook even the obvious.

A lot of people believe they are above harm, above trouble of all kinds. They may be fortunate, but the belief in one's own immunity to what befalls others is a false belief. Anyone who drives a car is subject to a flat tire. If you are driving behind a truck which is spilling nails on the road, you need to stop or maneuver around them. You may not see the nails, but failing to see them will not change their harmful effect.

Steel penetrates rubber, and criminals seek victims. There is no more attractive potential victim than the unsuspecting, or those blinded by their arrogant disregard of negative powers. There are many accidents on the road because people simply do not drive defensively. They assume other drivers are watching the road and being reasonably cautious. We know this to be untrue.

Zen Lesson: *there are universal laws, and no one is above them.* You will experience hunger and cold. So carry food, wear a heavy coat. If any human being anywhere is subject to life-and-death struggle, it's you. Caution is wisdom.

One Hand

So what is the power of One Hand?
Rudy Ray Moore said in a movie,
'I am so *bad*
I can put one finger in the ground and turn the
    whole world around.'

I was dizzy for days afterwards.
You can do this, you know.
You can spin the Earth with one hand.
Someone is doing it now, so
do you feel a little dizzy?

Not the little you.
The one your mother diapered
and pampered can't do such things,
but there is a you-not-you, but you nonetheless,
who can change the course of mighty rivers,
quiet a storm with an up-raised hand,
and alter history with a clenched fist.

There is such a you.
I speak of the you that the *Bhagavad Gita*
   sings of –
the one whom water cannot drench, fire
   cannot burn
and wind cannot dry out.

I sing not of the one who starts to perish the
   day he is born
but immortal soul that you are –
the Breath of God infused in form.
Inhale and feel your true nature
and lift your hand from there.
The moment it moves,
that movement is felt
throughout the universe.
Such is the power of One Hand.
This hand ... move it!

CHAPTER FOUR

SCAN MODE: DEVELOPING WARRIOR VISION

Most people are so used to their environment that they tend to superimpose their mental image of it over the scene. They see what they always see, even when things are different. The Zen Warrior cannot afford to cast an image over the real: he or she must go beyond the apparent to see clearly what is *really there*. This takes practice, focus and concentration. It is not enough to squint your eyes and tighten your brow. The power of concentration – *samadhi* – is more than physical exertion. When you develop it, you will raise the level of your game to unbelievable heights.

The Zen master Foyan said, 'Before your eyes is nothing but things that obstruct people.'

How can we put so much faith in what we call *seeing*? For certain we recognize colors and shapes, but do we discern movement, change and intent? After a session with my students one evening, I walked them out to their cars – it is something I like to do. I turned at the sound of growling and saw a man trying to hold back a Rottweiler. The dog strained against his leash and broke free to charge straight at me. Without thought, I watched him advance, as if in slow motion. I spoke to him softly, calling him 'Puppy', as I put my right fist behind my back. In a moment he was within reach of me, and there was a sudden change in his disposition. The little stub of a tail was wagging. He leaped to his hind legs and licked my face. His owner was so shocked he asked for my name.

This was not the first time a ferocious animal became tamed in mid-run. What no one knew was that, had the dog not changed his intent, I was ready to become the beast, myself. There is a sword that kills and a sword that saves. Given the option I will always choose the sword that saves, but I will not hesitate to strike when striking is expedient, to preserve life, limb or wellbeing – others' or my own.

When our understanding is correct, we take the appropriate action without hesitation. Petting the Rottweiler was a sermon in faith and peace. It is also indicative of the Way of the Warrior. Force should never be a first option. Peace should be desired above all else. Peace should be cultivated.

'*Budo* is love,' said Ueshiba Morihei, *O Sensei*, the founder of Aikido. *Budo* is the Way of the Warrior.

Love is a beautiful thing. I love animals, but I also love myself. I would not want to be torn to shreds. The Bible says that charity, meaning love, begins at home. There is no closer home than your own body. True love radiates from within you, then outward to others. If you are excluded from its nurturing power, it is not love but a form of delusion, a counterfeit version of the real.

Love sustains the beloved. Since the life of all beings emanates from the same source, each of us can trace our roots to that common source. Divine Spirit is the life of all.

Each of us must contemplate and accept that heritage for ourselves.

Since there is free-will, many are those who embrace the lower aspects of their being. Their behavior could be motivated by anything but love. As the growling Rottweiler charged at me, I first offered him the love I have for animals. He felt that, and there was no conflict. Unfortunately, human beings offer more resistance. A wagging tail may not lie but a smiling face can. Do you really *see* what is happening?

Years ago, I was lost. I was driving through a southern town in Virginia. I needed directions. I got out of the car, and I saw a group of young people my age. All of them were white and one was wearing a Confederate cap. Usually, close proximity to anything Confederate meant trouble for an African American like me. I focused, conscious that I may have to fight to make it back to my car. However, all of the young men were friendly. It was the one with the Confederate cap who gave the directions to me.

The incident prompted me to write an article on perceptions for the *New Journal & Guide* newspaper. I saw a hat and drew false conclusions from that. I knew what the symbol meant to me but not to him, so I asked him about it. His answer surprised me: 'It means I'm a hell-raising, fun-loving, beer-guzzling son of a gun.' It was a good learning experience. It is unwise to make blanket judgments. Each person, each situation is different.

Are you getting this? Are you *seeing*? Look beyond the obvious. Look deeper.

It is a basic teaching of ancient Zen masters that, in order to *see* directly, we must not rely on preconceived notions.

When we fill our minds with concepts and fixed opinions we cannot see beyond them. They will retard our responses and handicap us.

We have learned to attach a story to everything around us. It is easier to follow the story in our mind rather than to recognize *what is actually so*. For this reason we must practice throwing the stories out, emptying our mind. Just perceive, just hear, just feel. This emptying process is like dumping spyware and malware from your hard drive. Everything will function better.

I used to live on West 43rd Street in New York City, one block from bustling Times Square. One of my favorite places to sit and drink coffee was Nathans on 42nd Street. I became friendly with a man who always came in wearing a business suit. One night I asked him about his job.

'I go down the sink,' he said.

'I don't understand.'

'I pick pockets,' he clarified. At that moment my left hand involuntarily checked for my wallet.

'If I wanted to pick your pocket, I would never tell you what I do', he said. Then my new-found friend explained the art of the pickpocket, even to the point of telling me how he took rings and watches off people as they sat or walked. Fascinatingly, he was not a person you or I would suspect. He was well-dressed, friendly and chatty. Another lesson: *the threat may be disguised.*

A pickpocket can take your wallet or your jewelry because, at the time he strikes, you are distracted. If someone bumps you on the right side, you tend to look to the right. By the time you realize you're missing something, he is gone. Magicians use the same trick. It is called sleight-of-hand. Your eyes are focused where the magician directs you, while the real trick is being performed by the hand you do not notice. Such tricks are possible because, people being creatures of habit, their actions or reactions can be predicted to a large degree. But you do not have to be one of those people. *Are you looking where you are being directed? Stop that right now!*

To truly *see*, you must see with your vital essence. You must embrace your vulnerability rather than ignore it. The Chinese paper lantern is globally illuminated by a candle within it. Your awareness, your *seeing*, must be like that, shining through the 84,000 pores, as the ancients calculated. If you ignore your vulnerability, if you fail to remember that your skin is tender and your hair is flammable, you lack due caution in dangerous environments. This kind of awareness is twofold. It allows you to enjoy a gentle touch as well. Being aware through the 84,000 pores, you can feel the breeze flowing across the field or the shifting sand between your naked toes. Like a young child seeing the world for the first time, all things become brand new.

Some blind people can *see*. In the *Kung Fu* TV series with the late actor David Carradine, the blind master, Po, was amazing because he could fight as well as anyone who could see. In Japanese martial lore, Zatoichi, another blind master, used a sword with uncanny skill. These things may seem impossible, but it seems so only because most people do not discover how effective our other senses are in revealing the nature of our immediate environment. We rely so heavily on our eyes that they can blind us to other signals that are coming through.

If you had headphones on and your back was turned

to the door, you should still *see* that someone is entering your space. If you were attuned to your body, you could see with your skin. When the door is opened, there would be a change in air pressure, perhaps even a slight breeze or differentiation in the light. If you are in Zen Warrior mode, these subtle signs are enough to alert you that someone has entered the room. You will look around.

You have these abilities already, but you do have to awaken them. To help you do that, I offer a few simple exercises to stimulate the Zen Warrior in you. Katagiri Roshi, the Zen master, said, 'Everything I say is true. If this were not so, how could I teach others?' To benefit from these teachings you must receive them as if from that Zen master. There is but the One Mind, teaching through many vessels. I remind you: despite the image you see in the mirror, *you are not the body.* You use it. Accept this basic truth and we can move on.

In *Soul Sword: the Way and Mind of a Zen Warrior* I mentioned that a Samurai would enter a room as if the ceiling might fall in at any minute. He was observant at all times. Is there something out of place? Do you have a hunch, a premonition that something is about to occur?

Here's a Zen Warrior lesson: *if I walk into a room of 50 people and one person does not like me, the one person will attract my attention.* The other 49 are not a threat. I know the feeling of positive and safe energy. It is like being surrounded by family and friends. When something sends a different energy it is immediately recognizable as different. Thus, without effort, I naturally turn and look. It is similar to being in a room full of cats, all meowing at the same time when you hear a bark. What would you do? Most likely you would search for the barking animal. It is the only one out of place. Knowing the sound of cats helps you to discern what does not belong. Knowing the feel of comfort and safety can warn you when there is a threat to those very things.

The next time you are in the company of family and trusted friends, take a moment to sit by yourself and close your eyes. Tune into their voices but, more than that, tune into *them*. Feel what they are sending out to you through the ether. Feel what is coming to you through your 84,000 pores. Meditate on this feeling until you recognize it in your spirit.

Do this exercise in other places where you feel welcome and safe, even in your favorite public place. If you are a person of faith – that is, you consciously acknowledge the existence of God – it would be excellent practice to bring this meditation into your worship experience or church. In that way, you would become attuned to the highest aspect of your spirit. That will open you to a different dimension of sensitivity and response. I will discuss that more later. With practice you can take spiritual snapshots of your environment in moments.

There is a video game that shows a picture then repeats it with some differences. The gamer is suppose to see what has changed. The gamer needs strong powers of observation. That power to *perceive* accurately is valuable in everyday life. To know something has changed, we must have a good sense of what it was like before. If we do not pay attention to things and events around us we can fall into trouble. The unexpected is, after all, *unexpected*.

Not long ago, a family member of mine was walking across a semi-lit street. He took a step and fell 30ft down a hole. Someone had left the cover off a manhole. Fortunately, he lived through the ordeal. We expect, we assume that the sidewalk and streets will hold us up but, just as the ceiling could fall on the Samurai, the streets could give way. So much could happen.

There is a simple preventive exercise for this. *Watch where you are stepping.* Remember the feet meditation – feet have eyes, too. Let them step with care. We walk, we talk on the phone. We do so much. Are we scanning the territory? This will become natural to us if we practice. Then we will see danger and avoid problems as a matter of course.

You walk into a club or bar and you sense trouble from a person in the corner, so take note of it. Seek safety with your friends. Do not leave alone – stay aware. Do not confront the person. Nothing has happened. Do not fan the flame. In America, many ATMs are located outdoors. In my travels through Europe I notice that many of the banks I visit have their ATM machine indoors, accessible only to those who use their bankcard as a key. That is a wonderful safety feature.

People go to ATM machines at all times of the night, often alone, to deposit or receive cash. This is a terrible idea. Take someone with you, or wait until daylight, or leave early if necessary. Few people can turn away from punching numbers to fend off a robber at their back. Will the person just take your money or will they try to kill you? If you think they intend to kill you, then there is absolutely no reason to 'go gently into that dark night'. Too often, people comply and their reward is a senseless death. It is also senseless to be in an unsafe place at night when the business can be handled at a better time. My warrior advice here is: *avoid such encounters.*

Wisdom is the sharpest sword, and it is bloodless. Avoidance is magical ... poof! You are not there.

Scanning is an internal process. It happens when your combined senses penetrate the field around you but they alert you only when something is amiss. There is no strain involved. An airport scanner only beeps when it detects something that may be dangerous. Otherwise, it is silent. As you learn to trust your innate ability, you will be able to scan a room instantly without bringing attention to yourself. You will, to borrow a phrase from Samurai lore, have 'eyes like flashes of lightning'. You will notice what is important immediately. This ability will help others as well as yourself. It will also be an excellent skill to use on the job.

Look around you. What is out of place right now?

Lightning

Physically, they appear to be there
but a Zen Warrior has no eyes.
Let something suddenly move or change
and there will be two flashes of lightning
then thunder.

Seeing is not *seeing* unless it penetrates the seen
to the core.
It is not *seeing* until it receives the essence of the thing
    perceived.
It is giving and taking, listening,
feeling with the eyes.

The eyes of a Zen Warrior avoid danger before it
    occurs.
They see only the light
even if enveloped by darkness.

Opened or closed, there is no difference.
The physical evidence of eyes is not the eyes
of the Zen Warrior.
In spirit he never sleeps.
Because he never sleeps his eyes are always perceiving.
Eyes open, eyes closed,
do not pounce upon a tiger ...
Understand the nature of seeing –
wake up!
The Zen Warrior will never be caught off-guard.

CHAPTER FIVE

ONE HAND, ONE WAY

You've heard the sound of two hands clapping? *What is the sound of one hand clapping?*

If someone told you the answer, you may feel intellectually satisfied but it would be the same as dining on make-believe food. Here! Catch this! Did you get it or miss it? It is that simple. Is it working for you? If there is no transformation, no fundamental change, no awakening that affects your life, nothing has happened, no matter how much your vocabulary or intellect have widened.

Show me your hand. I am right in front of you. Show me your hand now! Seriously. If you responded to this command, even though I am not physically present, you are positioning yourself to receive lessons from a true master. That master, the teacher of all masters, is always present though not always manifest. The human teacher gives bodily form to him.

Now, for those of you who hesitated: extend your hand now! The hand you extend without thought is *your* hand. The other one, the left or the right, you must give up. Surrender it to the master, leave it to the unconscious. You will work with the one that you offered me.

Your hand is the one you engage in familiar tasks – you use it to hold your glass or cup or to manipulate a remote control device, or you move chess-pieces or caress the faces of your loved ones. This hand is your ambassador. Your chosen hand is an extension of your conscious mind: it does what you want and expect it to do. It is the ambassador of your will.

The *unhand*, the hand of the unconscious, of No-Mind, is like a secret agent. It is present but only marginally connected to your conscious mind. It is this hand that reveals the wondrous possibilities that lay within you, beneath the surface but not out of reach. Its operating system is the unconscious. When it works, the results seem magical, divine, unexplainable. Whether it is the left or the right, whatever hand you did not hold forth is now your 'sword hand'. This is the dedicated side of the Zen Warrior in you. It is this side that operates without conceptual thought, but you must learn to trust it. If you block it while you fish for an explanation or plan, you will never discover its power to aid you.

I discovered that I was a walking target after my book, *Kung Fu: The Master* (Donning Herschfield, 1975) came out. I entered a restaurant and heard a man call my name. He wanted to introduce me to his girlfriend. He had seen me on television, he said. I leaned over the table to shake her hand only to see a fist coming straight for my face. I caught his hand and held it.

'That was not very nice,' I said, and walked away. That my hand was there to catch his fist perfectly was amazing to me. Day by day I was learning about the power that had been unleashed in me. I did not know what was going to happen but *it* protected me nonetheless. This is what I want you to taste for yourself.

We go to school for so many things. Some of us believe that we cannot advance or know anything unless we have gone through a course of formal study at a university or trade school. We forget about those who are born with a genius for certain disciplines, who cannot be surpassed by the learned, but there is another type of genius recognized in Asia, the *meijin*. A *meijin* becomes a genius by sheer focus on his or her chosen path. Something occurs in their practice that takes them into realms unreachable by intellect or discipline alone. A transformation happens to them.

No matter what discipline this person embraces, he or she understands its nature as an experience. If the *meijin* is a musician his music will be flawlessly executed, penetrating to the soul. He will manifest the very essence of art as sound. While such a person may include formal study or embrace it later, his art will come from an unfathomable place unbound by labels.

It is this very passion that humankind has for labeling, packaging and boxing everything to neatly fit on the shelves that leads to unnecessarily restricted lives. More often than we may expect, it leads to unnecessary injury and death. It is time for you to use One Hand to break out of this trap. If you are to defend yourself like a Zen Warrior this next lesson is most vital.

Zen Warrior Lesson: *a white belt is all you ever need.*

You may think you are not qualified to defend yourself against an aggressor because you do not have formal training in a martial art. You may feel inadequate even if you do have formal training, because the bully who is threatening you has more. That person outranks you. It may be true that the person facing you may have more practice in a particular style of martial arts than you. They may even be a black belt in their discipline. We can applaud them for having the tenacity to stick it out and gain that consideration, but we owe them no consideration or admiration if they are planning on using that skill to beat us up.

We need to make a distinction here. The various martial disciplines are called 'arts' because that is what they are. The practitioner is taught to apply classical techniques in various situations. There is more to the training than fighting: there are forms to master, exercises to perform and tests to take. The student is measured against the ideal response put forward in the formal schools. Mixed martial arts pays far more attention to fighting, but the purpose of MMA is aggression, to beat the other guy. Even MMA has rules. It is a sport.

In reality, you will not be asked to qualify so that you can fight only against a mugger in your own weight-class. You will not be given protective gear, nor have a referee present to call the fight, if it gets out of hand. It will be you facing X, and you can do this. People can get hurt in a match, but there is no real intent to maim or kill. The referee's job is to maintain a level of sportsmanship, if not civility. In the real thing, life, there is no clock, no stopwatch, no referee. However, if you act from No-Mind, bringing forth the Unhand, you can come through this ordeal and escape harm.

What must change is the way you view yourself. At this point, what the aggressor plans to do does not matter. It is time to raise the whip on the horse again. You are facing an aggressor. Let's just say for effect that he is a renegade black belt – I say 'renegade' because most martial arts people are truly wonderful. Now, the only belt you have holds up your pants. Does it make you nervous to face an expert in Karate if you have no martial art of your own?

So what are you going to do? Stand there and let him punch and kick you at will, because you know nothing? Well, you do know something: you know how to receive pain. Believe it or not, if you can take a punch or kick and recover, you have the makings of an excellent warrior.

Before I had any personal experience of self-defense I would stand before a bully knowing he would hit me and simply take the blow. I tried to cover myself but I did not strike back. My attacker struck me over and over until he had had enough. The result was that I was in pain. Years later, when I was introduced to a class of warriors known as *Samurai* by Jujitsu master C O Neal, then a sergeant in the Portsmouth, Virginia, Police Department, I studied all I could about them. I was most impressed by the Bushido Code. I found martial techniques exciting, but I was more inspired by the philosophy. One powerful statement penetrated my mind: *when there is a choice between life and death, the Samurai always chooses death.*

An aggressor generates fear in his victim. The intended target may become compliant to avoid pain and suffering, but often pain and suffering are the very tools being used to create the desired result. Not wanting to feel pain is not a deterrent to pain. The person who punches you once may do so again because there is a sense of power he feels from doing so.

If you hit at a little child, most likely the child will hit back. This is an instinctive response unchecked by fear of consequences. It is this infantile state of mind that was prized by the warriors of old. If you walked by and punched your sibling on the shoulder, he or she was likely to turn and strike back harder, without even thinking about it. You had no business violating their space and justice was swiftly administered.

While we will naturally offer a defense against a mock or even a real attack from someone we know well, we can find ourselves frozen to the spot when a similar threat comes from a stranger. Introduce the unknown, the X-factor, and we are somehow clueless. We do not know what they will do to us, but do we therefore give them a license to harm us?

If you can avoid a confrontation, do so. But there are times when we cannot avoid facing a threat. It is during such a situation that we need a new attitude. The tough guy is standing before you shouting, his fist is poised to hit you and you are ready to receive it. If you could mirror the mind of a Zen Warrior you would open yourself to receive that coming fist, welcome it, without looking back for a place to hide. This is your conscious mind, your visible hand extended in goodwill … but you have another hand too.

By choosing to receive what is coming instead of running, you defeat the demon of fear. Fear weakens and paralyzes its victims but, when it has no place to take root, it becomes pure energy. That energy releases you from what binds you. One hand receives, the other hand gives. It is an act of nature like lightning, giving birth to the thunderclap which follows it. The Unhand is the hand of justice … *karma*.

My exploration of the Warrior Way came before my satori. As a result I can teach that you can heighten your ability to protect your space even without that wondrous experience.

In 1965, I was only 17 years old. I was living on my own in a rough Brooklyn neighborhood called Bedford-Stuyvesant. In Virginia, I had been mostly mild-mannered until the final months of my stay. When I left Virginia I saw the opportunity to change the way I carried myself. Since I had no history in the area, I fully modeled myself after the mindset of the Samurai. It was visible in the way I walked. It was not long before I was challenged, however.

This was a time when gangs ruled the streets of Brooklyn. I stood on the floor of the Police Athletic Center, so-named because the police sponsored it. Despite the name, the police were a rare sight at the center, and gangs seemed constantly present. A gang-member walked by me and, without any warning or provocation, threw a punch which slammed into my chest. Only a year before, that blow would have killed me or sent me straight to the hospital where I had already spent 16 months recuperating.

Feeling the pain rise up, I sprang upright and struck my attacker in his chest with all my might, but I used an open palm. He rose up in the air, flew backwards and crashed into a row of chairs, creating a domino effect that knocked down several rows one after the other. The noise startled everyone in the room, including the gang-members. That was my welcome to Bed-Stuy, but only the first one that night.

Fighting gang-members was never in my profile. I did my schoolwork, I went to Sunday school, I respected my elders and was a former Boy Scout. I had always been the boy running from troublemakers. How could I now be the one knocking a gang-member over rows of chairs? I received the blow consciously and felt the pain of it but, just as fast, like the stretched end of a rubber band, my other side lashed out on its own.

The effectiveness of the counter was that it just *came*. There was no hesitation, just release. I gave myself completely to the flow of the punch and the attacker fell. My other side, the Unhand, moved faster than the speed of fear. I knew nothing about the stranger. I did not even know whether he was armed. He struck me and I struck back righteously. Suddenly, the fear was on him.

It is important to have a white belt mentality, to know nothing but be open to learning everything, to be open to learning all the time. This is the virtue of the white belt mentality, that we learn, perpetually. We can learn and adapt, even in the midst of an incident.

The first time I ever fought a professional boxer I quickly realized that his power, strength and skill were focused in his upper body. At that moment, I decided to go to a place outside of this zone. I let him throw a punch, then I backed away slightly to avoid it, while dropping low to the ground. With one wide-spinning sweep of my right leg, I knocked both of his legs from beneath him and he tumbled to the ground. I was up by the time he struck the dirt, poised above him to strike.

I did not carry through on the strike because we were giving an exhibition. I learned that each person, each situation is different. We must look for a way to be revealed. Zen master Shunryu Suzuki spoke of the mind of an expert as being full, with little room to receive. The beginner's mind is the one full of possibilities. We must see the virtue of this mirror-like consciousness reflecting *what is*, but not clinging. No one can anticipate your moves if you do not know them yourself. It is possible to know nothing, yet to act with appropriate skill nonetheless.

People have become so accustomed to pre-packaged ways that they do not know that such an approach is only a shadow of the real thing. Genius in any field rises from within you, but it can be sabotaged. In this matter of defense, the aggressor we regard as the black belt brings a known factor into the equation. You, on the other hand, have the X-factor, in this case. What you know, what your skill is, is not known. If your mental attitude is right, you present the greatest possibility for success. To have the mind of a warrior and the continence of a warrior can take you much further than a headfull of techniques. To embrace the spirit of the warrior is superior.

By the time I was being written about in newspapers and magazines and appearing on television as the author of *Kung Fu: The Master*, people had pretty much decided that I was a Kung Fu practitioner, a martial artist. In fact, I was a poet and I was not trying to establish myself in martial arts. The title poem of the book was about the Way of the Warrior, but that was not my choice. The publisher made that decision despite my protests.

As I predicted, I became a target. In one incident I was on the Dick Lamb Show, on WTKR (then WTAR) in Norfolk, Virginia. I thought I was supposed to read my poetry. But the host came out in a *gi* (Karate uniform) and challenged me to demonstrate. I did not touch him but I eluded his punch, whirled low, spun between his legs without knocking him over and stood in front of him. This happened so fast that, if it were not for the cameras, no one would have believed it took place. As my reputation grew, it did not escape the martial arts community. They did not know where I fit into their world.

Master C O Neal, the police officer I met as a child, asked me whether or not I would agree to a test. I was tired of speculation about my ability or lack of it, so I agreed. Along with Master Neal, there were Soke Shiyogo Kuniba, ninth *dan* head of the Shitan-Ryu Sesshin Kai Karate Union, Hulon Willis, the seventh *dan* executive of AAU, and Masters Willie Hunter and Harold Hankins, both of whom lead different branches of Authentic Karate.

I entered the *menjo* as a white belt. More accurately, I did not even hold a white belt. I was just me carrying nothing more than a sense of the Warrior Way within, born out of a satori framed by years of probing the Mind of the warrior. I was ready to take whatever was brought to me to end speculation, and perhaps the constant assaults that were being made against me. Some fighters felt they would earn a reputation if they brought me down.

The white belt defeated each of the black belts one on one, then also as they attacked in groups. Every test was passed to the satisfaction of the masters. At the close of the day I was a black belt, the highest ranked black belt then in Master Neal's *dojo*. With my acceptance by the masters and my new found rank, I was placed in a key position in the BUDO Organization.

Master Neal did not treat me like a student. We had an alliance. He was deeply involved in the martial arts world. I brought Zen flavor to the community. When all had cleared, I was still just a white belt to myself. Everything I used that day rose from No-Mind, and it returned from whence it came. The only thing that made it all work, that gave some sense to what was happening to me, was that it was from Heaven. I was being guided, in the impersonal sense.

I say *it* moved. Still I know that the Master, proper, is a person as I am a person. He leads me because I know exactly how to yield. A white belt must first learn to trust the Master, then he must be obedient. The relationship is jazz, call and response. 'I give a command, so carry it out.' That is the lesson.

Without trust there cannot be the *guru-chela* (teacher-disciple) relationship. How can there be a *roshi* if no one responds? The lesson is for you. If you know that you know nothing, you can learn from everyone and every situation. The white belt is your symbol. You are wired to learn at each and every moment. You have already advanced.

The Hands of Time

There are ten delicious foods in front of you,
you can only have one –
there is no changing of your mind allowed.
Quick, grab something!
Are you hesitating?
There is a gun at your back: choose now or die!
What do you do now?

Slow or fast, you pick what you would choose
   anyway –
where is your faith?
Why must you be spurred onward by a whip

to move decisively?
Is pain your motivation?
Then let me strike you harder ...
Feel my hand pounding your head.
I am the clock,
You see my hands move but you can't stop them.
There is only one way to beat me:
feel the rhythm of my movements,
synch with me,
move as one with me,
use me,
then I am not your foe.
Use me, become me.
When it's your time,
you can move as you will
and you will be on time,
on target.
I move one way,
move one way.

CHAPTER SIX

THE *TANDEN*: CENTER FORCE

When we are working on an object located in space and time we must deal with it in a linear fashion. We can only speak of one thing at a time. Yet unifying is of vital importance if we want to get various and distinctly different things to work together as one. A car is made up of numerous parts – not just one of the parts is sufficient to get us along the highway. Together they do not create a greater but a lesser number: the many parts become one automobile. When we drive the vehicle our primary tool is the steering wheel for guiding it where we want to go. In a semi-conscious way we utilize the accelerator and brakes as called for. In this way, hands, feet and eyes work together, as one, without much ado.

This same ability, used every day by billions of people, can protect them off the road as well. The road or path of life goes everywhere, not just along asphalt trails. In a car, we rest, poised over a wheel, ready. We need a wheel when we are off-road also. There is no telling when we may need to guide the vehicle, our body, to a safe place. Unlike with cars, this movement is not dependent on mechanical tools, but we do need a steering wheel. Our Creator has provided us with a great one but it is hidden from the view of the ordinary person: there are many names for it, *hara*, *tanden*, abdominal region – all of these and none of them. There is a wheel.

When I was a child someone introduced me to the gyroscope. I was awestruck that it could maintain its balance in precarious situations. What I saw was a wheel within a wheel mounted on an axle and spinning with great force. Its centrifugal force neutralized the pull of gravity and kept bringing the tottering device back to stability.

We have a gyroscope within ourselves. Often people look at the size and weight of a person and mentally gauge their strength. They assume that the taller, heavier or more densely muscular person will emerge the victor in an encounter. If we use only the criteria of weight, height and muscular density, our assessment would seem about right but there are other more important factors to consider if a person is shorter, lightweight and lacking in muscle tone. As impressive as muscles may look, they are not in themselves the deciding factor in a conflict.

As a boy I loved Hercules movies, as played by Steve Reeves. But I was never able to develop even a pimple of a muscle compared to his biceps. That is why I was happy to see the emergence of James Bond – the skinny guy was the hero. Using wit and skill, he was able to outmaneuver and outfight all of his foes. That was the movies, however.

Real life brings with it real consequences. Our foes don't follow the script we want – they have their own agenda. What is most vital for us is that we have clarity about our own role and that we are at peace with our own position – we must find our center. When we find that center we can connect to it. If we lose it momentarily we need to know how to return and recover it.

You have a gyroscope within you. And you yourself are not the body. Your body is the axle, the pole the wheel spins around. The axle you see, the wheel you don't.

Gyroscopes are used in airplanes and spacecraft to help keep them on course. A gyroscope holds its position and resists any attempt to alter it. If it is placed upright on a piece of string, it will stay there. If you tilt it, it will stay in that awkward position, so long as the wheel spins. The wheel provides a counterforce against outside interference. Your center, the *kikai tanden*, the *hara*, the single-spot, has many names. The Bible speaks of living waters flowing out of the belly – this region of the body is given special significance.

Ueshiba Osensei, of Aikido fame, called it the 'ocean field'. Traditionally we place this spot in the region of the navel, one inch below it. Find that spot and press the tip of your finger firmly into it. What I want you to do is lock in on that location, *feel* it. Practice being able to locate it without your finger having to be there. For the time being, it's okay to employ your finger as a GPS device – soon you won't need that. When you can locate that focal point at will, you will have taken another important step toward your transformation.

Life brings many unexpected occurrences and storms – so many things trouble the mind and send tremors though our nervous system. Like a lake, when the mind is troubled it ripples and gets choppy, not reflecting properly. By *reflect*, I am not speaking specifically of thinking, but of mirroring. It is not able to discern what is. Just as the gyroscope remembers and keeps to its inherent position, we must do the same. If, like me, you have chosen a path of peace, you will never do anything consciously to contribute to violence or its contributaries.

We speak of the Spirit in terms like wind and water – thus we hear 'Ocean of the Spirit' or 'Wind of the Spirit'. The ocean is a visible manifestation of power. Its power is observable. The wind is invisible but its effects can be seen. Perhaps the ancient ones were speaking of two different attributes of one power. The ocean is far off but there is a pipeline that connects to it. Its starting place in us is that single point of focus one inch below the navel. It opens up to the vastness and matchless power of the Spirit.

We must choose a position in life. We might rely on our skills alone, our physical strength, or a weapon ... something. Your position is where you're coming from. I choose to position myself as a student of the Spirit – I want to embrace and be fueled by the Spirit. What I mean by 'Spirit' is what many people mean when they say *God*. That particular word has come to possess so much baggage, added by the minds of men – it suggests that God is a being as egoistic as man himself. I prefer the majesty and mystery of the Spirit, that which cannot be defined in any way by phenomenal beings, that which is beyond our intellectual prowess – that which dwells nowhere and everywhere at the same time, the personal and the impersonal, one but not the same. Because I position myself here in the dominion of Spirit, my gyroscope is so attuned that when I venture off course I am brought back on track.

If you rely on your muscles, you can tell when they are getting soft and flabby. If you rely on skills, you can tell when you have gotten rusty in the performance of them. To lose one's spiritual center is to fall into density from a place of buoyancy and light. When experiencing life from the focal point of the spiritual center, one has a body. When we fall from this awesome height we see and feel the difference clearly – in the fallen state, *the body has you*. Without the contrast of experiencing a spiritual shift, people do not know they are dragging a heavy package through the world. The ultimate warrior is born of the Spirit.

In the opening scenes of Bruce Lee's movie, *Enter The Dragon*, a *Shaolin* priest made this comment after seeing Lee, the character, do battle: 'Your skills have gone beyond the ordinary, they have reached a spiritual proportion.' The sword saint or *ki-sensei*, Miyamoto Musashi, became a great swordsman, then he went beyond that to the point where he no longer needed a sword – a wooden oar became his weapon of choice. Japan's Ueshiba O Sensei, founder of Aikido, also went beyond the normal range of martial arts to the point where he learned to employ *Aiki*, spiritual harmony, as his sword and shield.

Such achievements as these have long been associated exclusively with Asia. If we assume that they are limited to Asia, we diminish our spiritual standing to that of mere imitators. That center, that still point which points to the Waters of the Spirit is, indeed, within you. I know, because I was born in the West, yet I found it for myself. I did not know it was supposed to be limited to a certain geographical location or people.

I was not aware it answered to but a single name. I only knew that something was calling me, inwardly, and that it was the most inviting feeling of all. The yearning seemed like a message from home. This hunger in my soul came early in life, before the world's normal brainwashing techniques could latch tightly into my consciousness. My mind had no fixed perimeters. Since I had a prolonged period of innocence, there was nothing to block me from within. So I listened and I believed.

We often lose our center early. Being centered is when you are rooted, anchored in the true nature of your being ... Spirit. When that is so, everything else that happens to you in life revolves around that singular realization. All experiences are tested by this fire. Everything on Earth may move, but this is the immovable ... in Japanese, *fudo shin*, the Immovable Mind. Your sense of self is not an idea presented to you by others. You inhale and exhale yourself – *you*, in every moment, every situation. This is how you were as an infant: you needed no directions to express the universal nature of yourself as a child. It grew out of you spontaneously.

Finding the center means letting go of the images you see. These images are not *you*. Can you believe there is a you and a way that is traceless before it appears? Creation suggests something that appears out of nothing or nowhere. To make something is to use a pattern or pre-existing materials to form something else. Using the biblical reference, man was created. That means that the consciousness of Original Man has no past nor future focus. If that were true, he would not have a present mind either, since there would be no poles to create the contrast of this or that, past or future. In that way we can understand that the mind of Original Man is *No-Mind*. There was simply a functional consciousness that drew no attention to itself.

If that is hard to understand, consider that you are

breathing at this moment without seeing air. Air is carrying out its purpose in the background. Should you suddenly have to pay close attention to the air you are breathing, it would signal trouble. Your mind is like that. When it becomes the object of attention, the center is lost.

Mind and body function together like a hand in a glove. When you become lost in the mind, you are also trapped in the carnal realm. That is, you tend to interpret the world according to the data supplied by the senses. The sense world masquerades as the true world. It is not the true world, but if you haven't found a way back to the center, to the still point of your being, you will live your entire life as if in a soap opera.

A soap opera star may be great but he or she is a pawn of the script. No matter how good they are, their destiny is in the hands of the scriptwriter. They have no control over whether they live or die, or whether or not they will appear in the drama next week. The actor's fate always lies in the hands of others.

If you do not understand the importance of returning to your center, your life is like that too. The world and all the forces in it have different operating systems from our primal nature, but we hear the message of redemption faintly and without comprehension.

You are shoved around and tossed and turned by external forces because you do not remember or experience the essence of your being. The answer to your need is not found in your DNA, which is biochemical. The answer you need is not in words at all. You come to understand the answer by an overturning process that takes you into the experience. The prodigal child must return to the Father, but not everything will make it through the portal leading back home.

The world works on thoughts and concepts. These are needed to hold together the elaborate illusion cast before our eyes. However, if we want to rediscover the truth of ourselves as an experience, we have no need of thoughts or concepts generated by our own minds. These are figments of the mind, smoke figures. The truth itself is *alive*. It moves our eyes and wiggles our toes. The conceptual mind, for all its fascinating ideas, will never uncover the realness of *you*. It will only give you words and more words with which to talk and beguile others. The mind does not operate in the spiritual dimension – it is its own reality. What it knows of spirit is by secondary means, by reflection. The mind has no knowledge pertaining to its own origin. It just *is*.

Spirit is over mind, not the other way around. Consider this saying by a Zen master: 'Only when there is no mind in things and no thing in mind, only then are we marvelous, empty and free.' The freedom referred to is not something that someone from the outside grants you by decree, with a certificate. It is not the breaking of metal bonds. It is the unfathomable freedom of Spirit penetrating the whole of the universe, passing through all matter and barriers, being one with the Breath of God, the Breath of the Spirit. This cannot occur while the mind is leading the way.

Wherever the mind leads is only a projection of itself. It is like the holodeck on *Star Trek*. No matter how far a crew member traveled in the world created in the holodeck, no matter whom he or she met or the adventure he or she enjoyed, they never went outside the actual dimensions of the deck, neither did they meet anyone who was really there. Do you really want an inventive mind like this as your center?

The Bible speaks of 'the Word made flesh'. The Word came and dwelt among men. O Sensei also makes references to the Word in his explanation of the power of Aikido. In Japanese, *Aikido* means, 'the Way of the Spirit'. So the Bible points to Jesus as this spirit-centered man, the prototype for what we should be. When speaking of the powers attributed to Jesus, the Bible says, 'the Son, which is the mental being, can do nothing without the Father.'

Spirit is over mind, not the other way around. This was what was intended, but nowadays most of us are off-center, out of synch with our true nature, so we fail not only to see *things as they are* but also to recognize *what we are*. In this manner are we misled day by day, in many different ways. By not being rooted in the Immovable we are easily shaken by the storms of life – gusty winds buffet us.

When our adversary comes before us as a human being, they can be a triple threat. As a mirror reflects what is before it from the opposite side, so also is the nature of the adversary. He is flesh and blood, mind and spirit but, unlike the unawakened person, the adversary is conscious of his spiritual origin, rooted in One-Mind and strong in body. If you stand before such a one feeling uncertain, divided in consciousness and lacking in divine roots, you are in trouble.

We can battle a normal human being in our divided state, but we need an unbroken faith in the indomitable power of the Word to stand against a spiritually-driven foe. We are all endowed with mind, soul, spirit and the outer shell we call the body. When the saints, sages and masters speak of Spirit, they refer to the Holy Spirit, the active power of God in man – when the singer sings that the battle is not yours but the Lord's, it makes perfect sense in that context. In the Bible, David celebrates his skill as a warrior with this tribute, 'Blessed be the Lord, my strength, who teacheth my fingers to fight and my hands to make war.'

Were such gifts available only in the past? The believer recites that, 'In God there is no past, present or future.' This is familiar. 'Then' is 'now' to God. Such gifts are indeed available but we must meet Him in His secret place. He can only be present for me in that secret place. He can only be present for you in that secret place. These gifts, the centering that opens the secret gate, cannot be approached by mind or ego. Our brilliance will get us nowhere.

We have taken a journey, but we are still talking about the same thing, the *kikai tanden*, the *hara*, the abdominal region. It is important to understand that this is not a course in biology, psychology or the like – there is something far higher and deeper at work in the background. What you do, the steps you take, are like an offering, an act of faith ... just one step to plant the seed. The seed of faith is truly as small as a mustard seed. One inch below your navel, place a single seed. It sparkles like a diamond but it's just a tiny glimmer, a point of focus for your mind and nothing else. Reduce your thinking mind into this diamond seed, and wait.

The Psalmist says: *Those who wait upon the Lord shall renew their strength. They shall walk and not be weary. They shall run and not be tired.*

There is a story of an old master who walked, stooped over with the aid of a stick, suddenly being attacked. The old man stood up straight and defeated a band of attackers. Mission completed, he hunched over again and took up his walking stick. Such a story is easy for me to believe because I have experienced such a phenomenon many times. It is why I use the term 'Not-I' to distinguish between those things I did from my conscious ability and those that came wholly from the Spirit.

I have no explanation for or direct control over things that come from Spirit. It may look to others that I am in charge, but the truth is that I am not the lead dancer in such displays – I am shadowing the dancer. I am led through the forms effortlessly. If no one else knows, I am the one who knows that the Spirit is the Master – once again, hand in glove. By believing and receiving the gift, my body is the glove that gives substance to the Spirit. That relationship delivers me from the hands of my adversaries with grace and style.

I have spoken of the Ocean of Spirit within. There are great oceans out there in the world. They are magnificent and beautiful but they do not compare with the ocean we cannot see. We cannot see it, but we can *feel* the flow and the strength therein. The sea, the ocean out there, gives a mighty sonorous roar that echoes of eternity, but the roar of the ocean within is more powerful, yet it is strangely silent.

Our noisy, fragmented, discursive mind must become this ocean. It already is. You may feel that if your mind wasn't full of thoughts you wouldn't know you were alive and you might fall into nothingness. This is not the case. If you overload your computer it will become sluggish. It is like that with your mind. You cling to every thought and clog your memory with details. You do not believe that you can absorb what is useful and eliminate what is waste, just as your body does.

Instead, we have allowed people to tell us what is important, what part of our being should receive the most attention, and we have believed them. We have made the mind into a machine, a form of computer valued by marketplace standards. One mind is pitted against another, so conflict and contest are the order of the day because it seems we have no worth unless we are better or have more than the next person. But rest a moment: if you return to the place of refuge in the belly where the living waters of peace are said to flow, the nonsense will fade away. Your eyes will open up. You will see with clarity.

So sit in a quiet place and focus on the spot. Listen for the roar of the silent ocean. Just listen and do nothing more. There is no higher level of activity than that which is driven by the Spirit. Even the most mundane activity can seem like a religious endeavor. For that to happen, to go beyond the ordinary to the spiritual can never be a matter of simply quoting words or going through rituals blindly. Only that which comes from the Spirit is Spirit. Thus, the scriptures say: *God is Spirit and He seeks such as they who worship Him.* We must surrender our mind so that the core being, the spiritual, can return to Him.

Now this may sound terrifying. We might ask, what does it all mean? Where does it all go? Can I still function? It all goes nowhere because everything created has its own place from the beginning. Each vegetable can stand alone but we can also make soup of many vegetables. Only those with the most discerning palate will recognize what is in that soup.

The world has thrown you into a mental soup, into the collective consciousness, groupthink. Taking this journey within is akin to a pilgrimage up a sacred mountain to a hidden temple. You go because you are looking for something, for a transformation, but you do not know exactly what it will entail. When you come into Spirit, your Father will reveal exactly who and what you are because He will extract you from the soup and return you to your original condition.

This is a transforming experience. When we say 'God' and invoke scriptures, people naturally see things as smacking of religion. Thinking that, it is easy to become divisive and defensive. Most people who believe in God believe as a matter of course that the real God lives in their country and speaks only their language. However, if you believe that all human beings are the progeny of the same power, the secret of our nature and our restoration would lie with that same power and not with ourselves.

Connecting with the Father is a private matter. It is a direct dial-through to the source of our being, through the channel God gave us for that purpose – Spirit. 'And God breathed, and man became a living soul.'

I always believed the Breath of God was the life of man. Since I had that belief from childhood I was already pre-ordained to favor the Way of the Spirit as my path. I did not know then that it was a *path*, and in the broader sense it is also not a path – it is just life, itself. I suppose we designate it as a path, as a road leading out, because there are so many false roads to take. Countless though the false roads may be, only one path is life, and life is Spirit. That should clarify the matter somewhat.

By bringing your mind to this single diamond jewel below the navel, you will start the process of taming the beast that is your mind. Instead of following the constantly changing storylines of your thought-life, you will be working to bring it to a single point. Yes, this is Zen Warrior training for certain. Zen is not the exclusive property of a certain religion or sect. It is a tool for restoring the Original Mind, open to all who use it.

Bring that mind of yours to a single point. A sword comes to a keen point. Your mind will become your Soul Sword. With that sword you can cut the ties that bind you to the carnal realm. You will ooze Spirit and become truly alive.

Zen Lesson: think about this. *Zen is without thought.* You have just negated the practice. Practice breathing from the *tanden*. Do not think about why or how ... just breathe. Let the transformation come like a seed gives birth to a tree, without effort or conscious design.

The Sweet Smile of Victory

Standing before the adversary
you tremble
at the sound of his voice.
He is the beast your mother warned you about,
the one who hides in dark places,
the crusher of body and soul.
You tremble before his hollow eyes,
chilled by the cold wind of his spirit,
and then he moves closer.
You see his weapon already dripping blood
from a fallen one –
your brother, perhaps.
You tremble.
And then you remember something else your
    mother said:
Son, the battle is not yours but the Lord's.
And you believe ...
There is a rising within you –
it flows like a geyser through your soul.
You are not thinking of the adversary now,
You are rejoicing.
Like mighty David and Joshua, you shout
and the adversary trembles
when you smile.

CHAPTER SEVEN

DANCING WITH THE STARS

There is a popular television show in America called *Dancing with the Stars* – in Britain it's called *Strictly Come Dancing*. While you may never dance with the stars in real life, you should dance beneath the stars whenever you can. You can do that indoors. You can learn body coordination the hard way, going through long and expensive courses in martial arts, yoga or other forms of body training, or you can have fun as you naturally learn to trust and enjoy your body-mind. It is important to be comfortable with your own body. You do not have to look like a bodybuilder or model – you just have to learn what works for you. You have to learn effortlessness and you can do it effortlessly, if you follow this lesson.

Here's a secret. *The Zen way does not take effort.* Most people nearly kill themselves before they realize that their attainment had nothing to do with all the grunting and groaning they did. The Game of Life is fast-paced. There are many X-factors in the game ... unknowns that can surface without notice. Do we really have a long time to prepare for right now?

There are no shortcuts, but the long way is contrived.

In this dance you do not even need a partner. You will do nicely. The Samurai acts alone. The gamer, the Zen Warrior, faces the screen, faces the world, virtually alone. It is not the movements of the dance we are concerned with in this practice. The focus is on the mind of the dancer. In Brazil, enslaved Africans disguised a deadly martial art, Capoiera, as a dance, because martial arts were illegal. They whirled through the air in graceful movements that could break a man's bones with ease. They could fight without losing the rhythm of the dance.

In the West we worship the intellect, even when its calculations and examinations do nothing more than astound the listener for its sheer profundity. We recognize that the person must be superbly intelligent if we do not understand a word he or she says. The thinking mind has its own place in our lives, but there are times when too much thought, too much reflection, works against us. We become self-conscious and stiff, saying no to a lot of things.

Like music which can be written down and played note by note from a page, dance can be analyzed so that it can be broken down into steps and counts, 1-2-3, 1-2-3. A person who is counting off the steps may get all the movements correct but, despite his self-deception, he is not yet *dancing*. When the steps, the music and the count are experienced as components, something is missing. There is a dance but no dancer.

As a writer who became a professional in New York, writing for newspapers and magazines, I could have been considered an intellectual. Many of my stories were 'think-pieces', and I could move freely in intellectual circles of authors, scientists, activists and such. I could move in those circles but I could not move on the dance floor. I was top-heavy, too much aware of how I might look to focus on the feeling. In the vernacular of African Americans, I had no *soul*.

Well, I did have a soul but I did not express it. I resisted the feeling that wanted to move me because I was not sure what the outcome would be. I always fought to stay in control. Only after my awakening in the early 1970s did I go beyond just hearing the music. I felt it in the deep recesses of my being. Remember this: *when I resisted the feeling that was guiding me, I failed.*

Time can be calculated in many ways, as rhythm, intervals of space, pulsations and more. For there to be such a measurable experience there must be a means of measurement, a break of some kind. The cursor on your computer screen blinks. Because it blinks you can speak of it in relationship to time. If it stood perfectly still, time would not be a factor until you moved the cursor. Then you could say it was still for so many minutes.

All around you, every moment of every day, objects and people move about you in a rhythm ... so do you. The more aware you are of your own motion, the less awareness you have of that which is moving in the field around you. If you want to be able to move with grace at a moment's notice, you must learn to operate in a field of consciousness beyond time in the normal sense.

Remember, if you are always aware of your own movement, you stop focusing on the movement around you. As you master the teaching on finding your center, you will be able to look at your environment from that still point. It is like being at the center of a circle in which the

71

circumference is made up of living people. If everyone except one person or two is still, your attention will immediately focus on the ones that are moving. You will hear, see and feel the rhythm of their movement.

When you master the focus that keeps you tuned to your center, you will indeed feel the rhythm around you. That is the music. Do not shift your mind to your own movement or rhythm. Just listen to the music. Just as the dancer is one with the music, so must you be one with the external rhythm. As you practice, you will come to see that your body adapts to what is happening – an intuitive dance takes place. You turn, you look, you move forward or backward without taking awkward steps. Our way is effortless, natural. If you are awkward, hesitating and doubtful, you are not yet dancing.

Some years ago I gave a demonstration at an Aikido seminar in which I stood in the center while five martial artists attacked me at the same time. This was no practice, and they had never seen me before. In short order I threw each of them in sequence and I was never touched. You can find that video on my YouTube channel, *Kitaburoshi*. I did not know what I was going to do and I certainly did not know what the others would do, but somehow I was able to move through them in a perfect rhythm, to take them down and avoid the same fate. I was driven by the same inner-sense I am writing about.

You can tap that place also. When you find it you will sense a major change in yourself. Conflict becomes 'May I have this dance?' When the fear factor is gone we are capable of extraordinary feats. Getting beyond fear is a major accomplishment, but we should always remain cognizant that bodies are mortal and vulnerable. Being fearless is not the same thing as being reckless.

A dancer does not wait for a formal dance to ride the rhythm. Let yourself enjoy the range of movement and the creative possibilities available to you. That means dance when you're alone. Being alone, you can let yourself express freely. Dance! In this practice, the way you approach it is far more important than how you look to others. This is your dance. When you can move without effort from one position to another, when you lose your self-consciousness, you will be on course. In the next segment we will look a little deeper and offer some tips to help in your transition.

First, you must pause and relax.

We are told that we should let go, but the phrase 'let go', is not effective enough to help a person do it. In fact, letting go doesn't involve doing, it involves *non-doing*. This is extremely hard for people who believe that, if they are not active throughout the day, they are being lazy. Relaxing is important. By relaxing, I do not mean sleeping – that is something different.

Relaxing is something you can do effectively only while you are conscious. Cats do it very well. Their great cousins, lions and tigers, are also gifted in the art of reclining and letting go. They are powerfully explosive creatures, yet they can drape themselves over the ground without a care, seemingly oblivious to the dangers of the jungle around them ... they are relaxed but not asleep.

I have always loved music, but that love goes far beyond surface hearing. Music is spiritual to me. There is a type of music set aside for the purpose of worship and adoration that we call spiritual – gospel and hymns – but that kind of music is set aside to invoke spiritual feelings. The music I am speaking of is a different kind of spiritual music: it is laid between the lines and rhythms of secular songs. It is telegraphed to the soul of those who seek Spirit between the usual places and in unexpected ways.

The Master has no fixed address. You are not likely to find him in the Yellow Pages, under 'Master'. The Master only appears when you are ready. You are ready when you are willing to take the solitary journey that will alter your perception about the nature of things. A genuine human master confirms what has already been revealed in secret to you, in your own spirit. Thus, on making contact with a human master, there will be an unmistakable spiritual connection. Only then can your reorientation begin in earnest.

By reorientation I mean that your operating system begins an upgrade from being body-mind-centered to being Spirit-centered. Though long forgotten, this is our original nature. We do not want to admit it, but we have all been brainwashed – it was unavoidable. We entered the world as babies who knew nothing of its nature. What we learned of it we learned mostly from others, and not all of them had our best interest in mind. From the very first moment we understood a single word, we were open to the power of suggestion and manipulation. What hope of genuine clarity could anyone have without intervention from the only Intelligence who knows our true unspoiled nature? The answer is, no hope at all. The greatest minds of this world, bar none, function with egos rooted in the primal illusion. As you listen to them, keep that truth in mind.

Every culture in the world makes music through one instrument or another. Every culture in the world embraces dance. Dance is a part of the human experience. Long before I heard of Capoiera, the dance-centered martial art introduced by Afro-Brazilian slaves, I discovered a connection between dance and the Way of the Warrior on my own, during the disco era. What I learned may help you acquire greater fluidity, coordination and communication between your spirit, body and mind. The exercise is not a contest of any sort. It is something you do in private.

So let me tell you about war dancing.

If there is consistent movement, there is rhythm. If there is movement, there is timing. Movement creates intervals or space – both are aspects of time. If something occurs around us and we are reasonably aware, we will silently ask, *what is happening?* Then comes a pause in which we process the information, and then, *how do I respond?* Following that, whatever realization we have will cause us either to relax or to take appropriate action. The trouble is, if we actually go through these transitions in measurable time, appropriate action is highly unlikely. Responses to sudden events, when met in the tick-tock fashion, will be late and mostly ineffective. We can do something about that and enjoy ourselves in the meantime. We can engage in that universal warrior pastime and discipline, dancing.

You may be saying, 'But I already dance – I do ballroom, I do hip-hop, I am a Latin dancer.' Well, it is not the *type* of dance that you are doing so much as the *way* you do it that matters. Music contains the elements we need to teach our bodies a different way of responding to stimuli, to sense time and to move in and out of the rhythmic field that is all around us. The outer world provides stimuli: we must become the dancer.

A dance is what we do. It suggests a fixed reference or choreographed activity. The dancer, on the other hand, is a body of creativity and possibility, a person capable of expressing inspiration spontaneously through the medium of the body. A person who is 'doing a dance' has to listen to the music and then follow along – there is a difference between music and dance. But there is really no interval between the sound of the music and the movement of the dancer – they are seamless. They are one.

When break dance became popular it was easy to see that the dancers, not the music, were the point of focus. We watched their bodies in dynamic motion, but still we remained outside of their experience. The experience must be *yours*. Choose music that has drive and means something to you – that is, it has some inspirational or motivational impact on you.

Years ago I visited a friend's Karate school and observed as his students worked out to 'Rocky's Theme'. The pounding, adrenalin-pumping rhythm of the music inspired effort. The song was on a loop. The students gave their all to the exercises – the music lifted their energy.

I had lung damage as a child. I was keenly aware of the limitations of my stamina. However, I observed that, while some activities could tire me out quickly, I could dance for hours with no noticeable discomfort. During the early years when I was making the transition from pushover to Zen Warrior, I had to do battle with my self-consciousness. I was shy. I never mastered dances. I wanted to move *my way*, but other youths would criticize my moves because they did not fall within a recognizable category. When I was older, I felt moved to incorporate my martial sensitivity into the context of dance. As I moved about the dance floor, what I did amounted to *kata*, martial forms. They were disguised and not drawn from specific disciplines, but the spirit of the movements, the feel of them, was martial.

Allowing myself to use music to free the movement of my body soon showed me that we can re-program our behavior in an enjoyable and nearly effortless fashion. In the relaxed environment where people danced, I used the movement of their bodies to reposition my own. Gliding away, moving in. Rather than just being aware of the person dancing with me, I sensed the movement of the field. This is important.

When you enter a room or step outside, a possible threat may originate from a distance. It may not begin close to you. Being attuned to the rhythm of an environment, we become aware of that which is out of harmony also. This sensitivity doesn't just apply to movement but to the attitudes and dispositions of those around us also.

I was sitting at a lunch counter when the server made an effort to clean the space in front of me. She misjudged the distance. I heard a cry of alarm and looked up to see my coffee cup tilting over. Instantly, I rose up using the footrest of the stool, and pushed away from the counter with both hands, launching myself into the air away from the oncoming spill. I spun around to land safely on the floor behind the bar stool. In a moment it was over. Only I knew that the sequence had taken place without thought or effort. Not a drop of the hot coffee touched my skin or clothing.

The ability to respond in like manner is with you all the time. Zen master Bankei called it the 'marvelously illuminating Buddha mind'. I like to refer to it as our Original Mind, or by another name Bankei uses, the Unborn Mind.

This mind functions without interference or thought, doing its job without bringing attention to itself. Most people have no clue that such a marvelous reality is at work within them – they tend to ignore it. It is because of this lack of understanding about our fundamental nature that we can block its function.

The dance practice, especially when we are alone, gets beyond our inhibitions so that we give ourselves permission to move in different ways from the norm. Jumping off a bar stool and spinning around in the air is not normal. If I had gone through the thought process I would be aware of how the scene would look. That moment of hesitation would be sufficient for me to sustain a burn and ruined clothes. Fortunately, the Unborn Mind acted and it was finished.

This was a minor incident, as things go. However, if we habitually stifle the flow of liquid intelligence in small things, the dam will block the flow when it really matters. Dancing is not just fun, it is used in exercise programs also – warriors of old released their martial energy and strengthened the martial spirit through dance. It is all in how you approach it ... intent counts. If you approach your dance to free your body so that it acts in harmony with your will, you are making wonderful progress. When you can express your movements without plan, from the Unconscious (*wu-nien*), you will be approaching the extraordinary. Hear the beat? Feel the rhythm? Move!

Zen Lesson: *the music is pulsing through the room.* Do not think of what dance to do – don't be caught by a pattern described by another mind. Dance because you are the dancer and music is your Spirit expressing itself. Let the dance be whatever engages you, body and soul.

Now we should look into *sunyata* – the empty screen.

I used to live in the Woodstock in New York City, near 7th Avenue and 43rd Street. The area is the location for many movies. In *Spiderman*, the villain, the Green Goblin, flew around the Allied Chemical Tower, a building I could see from my window. I was privileged to watch the famous New Year's Eve Ball drop from its tower, from the privacy of my mock terrace. I was most definitely immersed in the city.

The Times Square area can be teeming with anxious, rushing human forms at most hours of the day. It's easy to lose one's humanity in an ever-shifting tide of faces. However, people can adapt to anything. Men and women who live in Japan develop a type of *samadhi* (concentration) that permits them to make space where there is none to be found – they go within themselves. New Yorkers have developed a similar skill – they can be alone in a crowd by choice. We can also get lost in a crowd easily – that is, we can lose our identity, or we can reverse the process to lose the crowd. We can see what we need to see and feel what we need to feel.

It is important to learn how to see the empty screen before we get trapped by the movement of the many forms playing out their roles on it. If we become attached to movement we can forget that movement was not always so. The frantic pace we have adopted, that we call life, is not the truth. We must learn to see the empty screen to become familiar with the peace and stillness that lies beneath the pace of the world.

The gamer sits before the empty screen before he loads the game. The warrior must *just sit*. Before opening the door and stepping into the storms of daily life, we must be reminded of the truth of our being. We sit, and through that sitting we come to remember with our inmost being what cannot be said. We sit, and that sitting is truly *shikantaza* or *zazen*, 'just sitting'. What was there before the first game was loaded? What was your life, before the world penetrated your mind? This answer can only come when we de-program.

This can be a paradox. If you do not remember your life before the program started, how will you recognize it as true when a breakthrough occurs? For that, there is, as my book *Soul to Soul* reminds us, a factory-authorized technician to return us to the 'original factory settings'. This is the work of Zen masters and gurus, though they may be known by another title. They treat the disorder of minds with *Dharma*. Dharma is medicine for the consciousness, but the bottle is empty. Dharma is not a fixed reality. It is liquid. It blends well with 21st-century technology and humankind today.

Let us take a closer look at the empty screen, as it pertains to the scope of this book, awakening the Zen Warrior in you.

A mirror holds no image. It reflects as if not reflecting. There is nothing in it, after all. The contents of an empty screen can be seen at once – no effort is needed to monitor it. There is no coming and going. All is at rest. This is your true nature, natural and free. It is nothing extraordinary. It is simply what it is. If, suddenly, something appears on the screen, you will immediately notice it. Without any adjustment of mind, you will know whether it is red or blue or mixed in color. Your mind needs no special training to do this. This is your marvelous Unborn Mind.

It is easy to see the active world with its cars and planes, its crush of buildings with streams of people going here and there. With such powerful distractions it is no wonder that we miss the most marvelous presence in this world. As our senses scan the apparent world, we miss our own genuine self. This self, like the Unborn Mind, cannot be visualized or crystallized in any way but, without it, the universe is void, with no consciousness to recognize its absence.

Nothing needs to be added to the screen. With our imagination we create the villains who make us tremble. With our thoughts we bind our hands and feet so that we are powerless to act decisively. No ... nothing needs to be added to the screen. We need to empty it by the process of emptying our mind. 'From the first, not a thing is,' reads a Zen teaching.

It is akin to the declaration in Genesis which tells us, 'In the beginning God created the Heavens and the Earth.' From that scripture we discern that there was a time when there was neither a Heaven nor an Earth ... and God? He is without form or substance, one who is beyond explanation and definition. God is the greatest of all *koans* (spiritual riddles) – any words or ideas we keep in our mind about Him reduce our chances of unity with God. Even to say 'Him' is problematic.

In the same manner, if our mind-screen lingers with the images in front of it, locking in on ideas and thoughts about all we see, we become prisoners of that limited dimension of consciousness. We become trapped in the box ... the Matrix. Our ability to act or respond to circumstances is severely limited because we will have reduced ourselves to a concept.

Consider for a moment *Star Trek*'s holodeck. The computer-driven, holographic movie-sound stage generated worlds and peopled it with any characters desired, from the most beautiful woman to the most vicious villain. In such a rich environment, it is easy to get lost in the adventure. It is important to remember that none of the other characters or scenery in your life is really real. You cannot put faith in what you see. The holodeck, for all practical purposes, is always empty.

'From the first, not a thing is.' As a Zen Warrior, I realized that there was no opponent to be found. This is a paradox. If there is no opponent, no enemy, then who are we defending ourselves against? A falling branch is not an opponent or an enemy, but if you are under it you will be struck all the same. Like videogame characters who have no movement or substance outside the monitor, bodies have fixed properties that respond to predetermined signals or conditions. We feel heat and cold, hunger and pain, pleasure and annoyance. All of these are human responses that can be felt by humans around the world.

As the monitor displays what is generated by the central processing unit (CPU), your mind reflects on what is projected by the hardware. In the larger sense, the world itself is the hardware. We come to see our projection as the real world and what we experience through it as reality. But remember that computers, even bio-mechanical ones like our bodies and the Earth, are programmed. Seasons come and go, the sun yields to the moon, salmon spawn after an arduous journey taken season after season ... there is a program in effect. The question is, are your responses programmed too? Can you act in a different way from the way that has been set for you? Who is programming you? What can you do about it?

If the screen of your mind is always filled with characters and stories told by others, you will always be a minor player in life. The screen is empty now – there is nothing on it yet. Who are you at this moment? Do you know that the attitude of your mind determines the quality of your action?

So taught Shunryu Suzuki Roshi in *Zen Mind, Beginner's Mind*. I quote the statement because my own experiences bear witness to the truth of it. For me, the transition from victim to victor began when I ceased to believe in my powerlessness and assumed the role of a Samurai. I didn't just think about it or read books. I didn't wear the garb, nor did I carry a sword through the streets. I observed the bearing of such magnificent Asian actors like Toshiro Mifune when he reflected the essence of the type. I tasted the spirit of such warriors through movement, demeanor, voice. When I saw Mifune's portrayal of the Samurai in *Red Sun*, it spoke to me. I knew then that if I wanted different results when I walked through the streets, I had to change the way I presented myself to the bullies who challenged my peace. Something had to change. It had to be *me*.

At that time in my youth, the images on the world monitor were not flattering to black men. A history of wholesale abuse and legal bondage did not combine to make black men appear heroic role-models. Watching Toshiro Mifune battle white men without fear or hesitation was empowering because, in the American South of the past, the very attempt to raise a black hand in self-defense against a white man would result in lynching. That was a powerful deterrent. That system-supported prohibition against black manhood routinely produced a passive response amongst black men to abuse. Failure to act where warranted cut deep into the soul.

I saw something I wanted in myself. My new life, my new attitude, began when I embraced the likelihood of pain and possibly of death, instead of living my life in fear. It was obvious to me that there was no other choice. The Samurai model offered me a clear alternative. For a boy seeking healing for the soul, the medicine which came from Asia was like using a healthy left hand instead of a wounded right. The choice was natural. It was there for me. I had no philosophy, nor any need to cite references for my decision, but I sensed the rightness of that decision for me.

The Bushido code began its work on my consciousness. 'I have no friends. I make my mind my only friend.' I had a far more serious reason to cultivate the Way of the Warrior than avoiding school or neighborhood bullies. My life or the life of one of my loved ones could depend on my actions. I was determined to conquer my fears. The screen, the field, gradually became empty of pre-set images and, with that, pre-set responses.

Courage began to radiate from my *tanden*. It was not directed at anyone or anything in particular. It was just a feeling which flowed globally through and from all parts of my body. It was as if my body was emitting light in all directions. Once I could feel this power working in me, I could walk with confidence and focus. With each step I took, the Earth shook ... or so I felt.

The universe expands in all directions from where you stand. Meditate on this. Your body will follow your mind. The body does not act independently of the mind. Consciously or unconsciously, the mind is at work in all that we do, all we experience. We can allow the inflow of information to enter our lives, and we can leave our response to chance, or we can teach ourselves to respond to the known and the unknown in a positive way. So we take up the whip and crack it in the direction of the horses ... the mind.

There are certain teachings that must be taken on faith. If you read scriptures, doubting their veracity, they will not help you. As a boy, I learned to trust in whatever I was led to by the Spirit. I did not accept everything a person said to me but, if I was led to the study, to a book, an article or a person, I accepted it as gospel.

When I was a young boy, not yet a teen, I went to the theater to see a horror movie. It was worth the money because I was filled with terror and jumped from my seat to go to the lobby, to escape. Later the theater lights came up and the screen was white – there was nothing on it. Not a goblin, ghost or demon in sight. In truth, when the images ran back and forth across the screen they could go no further. They only *appeared* to be living threats. However, my mind had taken them as truly real, and I had responded that way – scared. In like manner we often respond to an image, to an imagined outcome, as though they are real. As a result, our mind produces an improper response. The poem below reminds you of the fundamental nature of thing-objects.

Zen Lesson: *fear is a response to a preconceived thought, not to the object before you.*

The Empty Screen

There is nowhere to move:
you are bound
and trapped ...
The words hold you,
the five colors lock you in ...
You inhale but there is no room to breathe.

Close your eyes ...
what do you see in the void?
How deep is the world now?
Forget the words for this and that.
There are no colors to see,
no crowd to block your path.
Do you know that you can run
and there would be nothing to stop you?
There really isn't anything or anyone to stop you.
You are simply
believing a lie ...

Now open your eyes and run
with all your speed
and all your might.
There is nothing in your way,
no wall to collide with.
All is empty, after all –
just projections in the air.
Run into the bosom of the One,
you are already home.

CHAPTER EIGHT

REPROGRAMMING YOUR BRAIN: THE BUSHIDO INITIATIVE

I came across the following verse the way I came about all of the teachings. Without looking, I discovered it and knew it was meant for me. I read it believing that if I practiced the teachings, they would bring the desired change in me. I was excited. I include it here in hope that it will trigger in you a sense of excitement.

No one has to be a victim. There is ample power within us to shield us from danger, if we would only learn how to release it. By now you understand that it is how you use your mind that determines the quality of your responses to life's situations.

There is a mystique surrounding the Samurai warrior. There was poetry in the way they carried themselves and faced life-threatening situations. The work I discovered as a boy was part of the Bushido Code. The verse below reflects the attitude and mental state of the quintessential Samurai. If you read it as the rendering of a poet it may sound good to you, and quotable, but it will do you no good. You must internalize, invoke. It must be you saying each verse with conviction.

There is no need to don the armor and carry the *katana* of a warrior through the modern streets of today, but there is a need for an equivalent, as you will come to understand.

The Mindset of a Warrior

I have no parents;
I make Heaven and Earth my parents
I have no friends; I make my mind my friend
I have no enemy; I make carelessness my enemy.
I have no armor; I make goodwill and honesty my armor.
I have no fortress; I make my Immovable Mind my fortress.
I have no sword; I make my surrendered ego my sword.
I have no magic; I make submission to Divine Will my magic.
I have no miracles; I make the Dharma my miracle.

CHAPTER NINE

I HAVE NO PARENTS; I MAKE HEAVEN AND EARTH MY PARENTS

Human beings are born by means of a mother and father. Right away the question is raised, 'How can a person exist without a mother and father?' The real question is, *how can a person be a person if he is born of a mother and father?*

The statement, 'I have no parents,' points to our Original Nature. Man is not mere flesh and blood. Man is born of the Breath of God. He is the immortal soul, sings the *Bhagavad-Gita*. The would-be Zen Warrior embraces this truth.

It may start as a mere belief but we cannot be a Zen Warrior until we experience for ourselves the Unborn Essence, *muga* (Japanese), no self from which this mortal self is derived. Some people call themselves 'children of God', but they are carnal (flesh-centered). God is Spirit. Any child of God would share that attribute. He or she would be Spirit-centered.

God's mind is No-Mind, untraceable. His children also possess 'No-Mind'. This is not to say that children lack a relationship with God, but the relationship will not have the maturity of an adult child who has earned independence. The Zen Warrior, having no mother or father (no center in the flesh) functions from the eternal security of spirit. This flip in orientation is vital for the next step of transformation.

The height and weight of our parent's child can be measured in mathematical terms. The likeness of our ancestors can be seen in the shape of our head, the curvature of our nose. This is our linear identity. It is kept locked in our consciousness by the governments and other institutions of this world. This identity is a product of thought.

Our Original Identity has no past, nor does it have bodily form, yet it can synch with the body as a hand can synch with a glove. If you believe you are the body, your mind mirrors its vulnerability. Example: the glove catches fire. Forgetting the true nature of the glove, you run about screaming. If you remember that the glove is not your hand, you can pull it off and cast it aside. Your hand will remain unharmed.

When we identify with the weaknesses of the body it is easy to be fearful. When the mind is focused on 'No-Thing', it is open to endless possibilities. 'From the first, not a thing is,' Zen teaches, but that teaching is not unique to Zen. 'In the beginning, God.' The offspring of God must be of the same essence of God. You are not a thing. You are not the flesh. A Zen Warrior can be nothing less than a Child of Heaven.

People tend to think in broad terms but, if you would unleash the truth that is buried within you, you must choose the narrow road. This road is so narrow that only one person can walk it at a time. The teachings, Dharma, have the purpose of freeing you from a trap that binds you, body and soul, to an elaborate system of lies. If every person in the world drank water except you, you alone would be thirsty, until you took a drink of the life-saving elixir.

Each of us who takes this road to freedom must do so for ourselves. We take one more step away from the carnal view of ourselves and embrace the spiritual reality. We have no parents. Heaven and Earth are our parents. Saying this, even believing this, does not mean you have to call your mama on the phone and tell her she is not your mother. Embracing this teaching is the recognition of oneness.

Though we are many numerically, each of us remains one life, one experience against the backdrop of the universe. To experience the true nature of your relationship with the whole, you must in effect become Adam, the first, the only man. The Earth was Adam's mother and Heaven or God was his Father. Here was the soul expanded to the farthest reaches of the universe. This is man.

To lay comfortably on the bosom of the Earth is to be fully at home upon the planet. The Earth is the body of Mother. Her spirit is spontaneous, free, unpredictable, but she is the provider for her child.

Reaching up, the man is at peace with the unfathomable mystery of all, because his spirit bleeds into the Spirit, which is after all his Father. Born of the marriage of Heaven and Earth, the man is the manifestation of Mind and Spirit, containing both, clinging to neither. He freely roams here and there, at home everywhere he treads. This is who you are. Where is the place where such a person can feel uncertain? Your Mother is the Earth. Your Father is Heaven. Embrace them.

CHAPTER TEN

I HAVE NO FRIENDS; I MAKE MY MIND MY FRIEND

Years ago I heard a story about a man and his son. The man placed his little boy on top of a dresser. Standing precariously on the high piece of furniture, the boy looked to his father.

'Jump!' the man said. 'I will catch you.' With the faith of a child, the boy launched himself into the air only to fall heavily upon the floor. Crying and wiping his eyes the boy stared in disbelief at his dad. 'You didn't catch me,' he wept. 'Let that be a lesson to you, son. You can trust no one.'

That story comes from Western tradition. Here is one from the East.

A master thief thought it was time to teach his son the craft. One night he took him out on a job. The target was a big house. They slipped into the residence with no problem. As the boy looked about for valuables his father made a loud noise, unbeknown to his son. Knowing the residents of the house would now investigate the noise, the boy looked for an avenue of escape.

'Get in that trunk', his father said. As soon as his son curled himself into the space, the father shut it and locked him in. Then he quickly slipped away without being noticed.

Later, at home, the father heard his son enter. His son was angry. 'Why did you lock me in that trunk?' he asked. 'Never mind that. How did you escape?'

The son sat down and explained. 'I heard people running around the house. I knew someone was near the trunk. I could see a flickering candle. I made a scratching sound like a rat. One of the servants opened the trunk. I quickly blew out the candle, shoved the servant aside and exited through a nearby window.'

The father was proud of his son. 'You have mastered the art,' he said.

In the ordinary world, letting your child fall or placing him or her in danger would be a form of abuse. For a Child of Heaven – that is, anyone who would taste Zen experience – it would be cruel to shelter the child. We are not addressing the ordinary way of looking at things here. This path is by nature extraordinary and the rewards of walking it are immeasurable. It is attainable, but the method of so doing is more triggers than principles.

You turn around and an object is hurtling through the air at you. With only a fraction of a second to act, what makes it possible for you to maneuver out of the way, deflect it or catch it, instead of being struck? What decides in that instant what action is appropriate? Suppose your reflexes are so fast you can catch a falling object without blinking … but it is a hot iron. Reflexes are not Zen. Real Zen is *prajna paramita*, instinctive wisdom. We cannot fake wisdom, and knowledge operates in the field of time. Here's one more story along this line.

The *Mumonkan* collection of *koans* tells the story of

Gutei. He was a master that used one finger to indicate his Zen. He would answer the most profound questions about Zen by raising his index finger. A young student began imitating the master when it came to matters of Dharma. He raised a single finger when questioned about Zen. Gutei learned of this. One day he asked the boy a question and he instantly raised his finger. The master grabbed it and cut it off. The boy dashed away in pain and terror but Gutei called out to him and asked him to demonstrate his understanding. The boy started to move his finger but it was not there. At that moment he was enlightened. The lesson here is not about mutilating a child, but the message is as sharp as the blade which cut through the offending digit.

If you are satisfied with mediocre living and uninspired responses to life's situations, then by all means, learn by rote. Today, anyone can sign up for a black belt course. Put down money, do the prescribed practice, learn the fixed routines (*katas*) and spar (*kumite*) in a controlled and protective environment, and earn the once-coveted black belt in a charted number of months.

Decades ago, before martial arts became a big business, the *sensei* took great pride in producing students who could really use the art. Today, that is not entirely true. Many people are learning no more than a martial ballet. They would fail in a real encounter because their mentality is not geared for actual live combat situations.

I was greatly disturbed some years ago when I heard that a second degree black belt from Japan was stabbed to death on a New York Street. I had the idea that the man would be a superior fighter because he was from Japan, but people are individuals. Martial arts is part of Physical Ed in

Japan, much like basketball, volleyball and other sports in Western cultures. People can give a passing performance in a secondary school program that would not be acceptable in a school dedicated to martial arts. It is likely that the victim was not a warrior at heart. He could not perform as such on demand.

In any controlled situation, there are coaches, references, checks and balances. There is someone to say, 'stop!' These are 'friendly powers'. A mind that expects help, looking for a rescuer, is divided, looking back and forth and over his shoulder for the helping hand. This is not good. The boy who jumped from the dresser thought his father would help him. He did not control his fall.

The young thief was angry with his father but there was no help to be found. He concentrated and a way was revealed to him. He relied on his own mind. Gutei's student did not seek to penetrate the real secret of Zen – he simply copied the master. When his crutch was taken away, he had no easy help to call upon. Suddenly, his own way was clear.

In the modern world we are trained to rely on many agencies and machines to act on our behalf. But what if there is no one around? What if the machines fail? When I was in college I worked in a restaurant. One day I tallied a man's check and he challenged me about the amount: 'I want to see that on the calculator', he said. 'You did that too fast.' I took up a calculator and put in the figures and showed him the answer. It was the same.

'I am surprised that you could do that.'

'Before there was a calculator there was a marvelous device called the mind,' I said.

I practiced doing my own tallying because, one day, I

asked myself what I would do if the batteries in my calculator were dead. Would I panic when a customer came up? Right then, I decided to do my own numbers.

All of these examples point to the same truth. We should make our own mind our friend. 'I have no friends: I make my own mind my friend.'

Sure, there will be people in your life ... friends. However, this is a discipline that purports to open you to higher realization. So in practice, as a matter of course, you must act as though there are no friends, no rescuers. Your mind is your friend, your backup. You will never experience what the mind is capable of until you take away the crutches that cripple it.

No help is coming, so escape from the trunk. No one will catch you, so land softly. There is no answer to the fundamental question that anyone can give you, so answer it now without hedging. When your mind is your friend it is always on your side. When the unconscious and conscious synch, your life is electric. This friend is ever-present.

When your mind is your friend you will always act in your best interest without hesitation. Out of this experience flows life-affirming wisdom.

Friend

I looked high and low for one to call my friend.
I saw people everywhere
but none were there for me.
I needed someone to feel
my deepest concerns,
to share my dark secrets
but never utter them aloud …
I needed someone who lived for me,
breathed with me,
someone to walk with me all the days of my life,
to cry and laugh with me …
I needed a defender
whose sword was ever raised
but whose smile never faded.
I searched but never found such a friend.
I never found him because he was never lost,
My friend is the Lord,
and the Lord is One Mind
without beginning or end.
From birth through eternity
I am never alone …
Where there is one
there is the other.

CHAPTER ELEVEN

I HAVE NO ENEMY; I MAKE CARELESSNESS MY ENEMY

It is not a good idea to put a frozen mask on 'the enemy'. If you make the mistake of expecting the enemy or assailant to resemble a certain ethnic group or wear certain identifiable clothing, you will be terribly surprised when someone who does not fit that profile brings a problem to your doorstep. The enemy has no face. There are crisis situations and a need for action, but it is the situation itself, not the person, which is the focus of the warrior. When you concentrate on the situation you transcend personalities.

There are many persons with malevolent intent, but it is not their intent which does harm to others. An intent is just a thought that can remain in consciousness. It is the act, energy released in this world, that causes effects. You must intercept that energy in some way, effectively neutralizing its intended purpose. You don't have be of Rambo proportions to do this. The smallest unexpected response can change things, but nothing is a greater ally than caution and awareness. You must practice it everywhere you go. It is a game of sorts, but the payoff could be your health, wellbeing and life.

We should be able to go anywhere safely, but the truth is that there are adversaries to peace. They are active on the spiritual plane but they really hurt us in the body. Human beings are excellent agents of these forces. You may be familiar with the Japanese word, *ki*. It represents Spirit or the energy of the universe which flows through us. *Ki*, however, is not just positive. There is negative *ki*. If you are familiar with positive *ki*, you should be able to discern the presence of the opposite. That would be very helpful.

You walk into a pub and in moments you feel uneasy. It is a feeling you cannot cast off. It is time to leave. It does no good to acquire such sensitivity, only to ignore it. To acquire this kind of ability you must first recognize that it is already present. You must penetrate the layers of distractions which keep you from experiencing its warnings and signals. You can do that by taking time out when you enter a place, to be silent and to focus on nothing in particular. Like sand settling to the bottom of a still glass of water, discursive thoughts will fade and you will know things in a different way.

We expect our days to be largely uneventful, so we do not have our shields or swords within reach. Shield and sword are symbols of caution and defensiveness. When the biblical warrior Gideon was told to choose his warriors, God ordered him to choose only those men who did not lay down their swords or shields to drink water. These were true warriors. They were in their own camp, but still they were ready.

Each of the segments of this book interlock. One teaching gives rise to another. Your mind is your friend and protector when it is able to intercede unconsciously, to act as necessary. It is the sword and shield blocking an unexpected sword thrust, instantly. If you challenge this activity consciously, in order to examine or censor the action, you are already cut down.

The communication must be like an old Zen saying called 'Flint striking steel': *Flint is struck ... then the spark.* There is nothing complicated about this ... except you were made this way, but do you trust in the way you were made? We have become so accustomed to knowing things mentally that we find it difficult to allow the primal wisdom, *prajna*, to be the decider. Failure to trust in our Original Nature leaves us prime targets for roving adversaries.

On January 9, 2011, Americans in Phoenix, Arizona were going about a normal weekend of activity. They were shopping in a mall. Some were listening to their Congresswoman, Rep Gabrielle Giffords, give them an update on her activity. One of the observers was a nine-year-old girl named Christine. Within moments a 22-year old college student walked past the others, pulled out a semiautomatic handgun and fired repeatedly. The Congresswoman was struck in the head, the nine-year old was slain. Five other people fell dead. Many more were wounded. In the few moments of bloodshed when bullets struck randomly, one man shielded his wife with his body – she lived, he died.

There was an unexpected lull – the shooter needed to reload. With selfless presence of mind, two men dove upon him and wrestled him to the floor while a woman grabbed the ammunition clip. The shooting was over, and the suffering began. Who would suspect Jared Loughner, a college student, of being a mass-murderer, a would-be assassin? We should expect the unexpected.

While nothing can be done to change the outcome of the aforementioned tragedy, we can use it as a model to learn. I offer respect to those who acted to prevent greater bloodshed and a deep bow to the man who became a living shield for his loved one. That was true love. The question is, how would what we are learning here make any difference?

The difference depends on your disposition and orientation. If the bent of your practice is self-preservation, you will have succeeded if you are not harmed or killed during a skirmish. Such a focus would of necessity suggest various options. Your physical body comprises the danger zone. It inhabits limited space. If you have practiced well, you intuitively grasp the range of your body.

Seeing the weapon, you instantly understand its nature. Danger comes from the barrel. It must be aimed at you. Stay out of the trajectory, put something between you and the gun – a chair, a column, a door ... stay low and move without looking back. Looking back is dangerous because it slows your pace and can generate greater fear. These are only suggested scenarios because what we do arises spontaneously and is not the product of strategy on the conscious level. The effectiveness of such action is that it is as unpredictable as the assault itself.

If you are concerned with saving your loved ones you will have your attention on them, providing yourself as a living shield if necessary, to guide them out of the way of danger. Being concentrated in such a way, fear will have no power over you. Your focus is the safety of those you love. That would be your success. You may survive this single-minded action, and that would be wonderful, but if that is your primary goal you will be like the preceding person.

The two goals, saving yourself and protecting others, are not mutual at the conscious level. A natural conflict arises and the mind will become divided.

The divided mind is not your friend. One Mind is not to be achieved in the practical sense – we speak of it metaphorically. It is in the doing that marvelous activity takes place. By concentrating on one act, all of your available energy is dedicated to a single mission. Concentration, *samadhi* (a Sanskrit word), is the bridge to enlightenment. It makes extraordinary deeds possible.

Then there is the Way of *Budo* ... the Warrior Way. If this is how you express yourself, as a police officer, a soldier or one with that kind of mentality, your sole concentration will be on the attacker. You will seek a way to bring him down. You will not try to escape: your mind will be pointed forward. You are like the one who shields his loved one, except you are everyone's shield. You want to end the threat. Just as a shield can be a door, a chair, a column, anything that provides protection from a shot, you may not be armed but that does not mean you do not have a weapon.

In a demonstration I took a cocked gun from a student before he could pull the trigger by tossing at his feet the book I was carrying. Startled, he reeled back. In that moment, I closed the gap between us and took the gun from his hand as I threw him to the floor.

Each circumstance is different but, if you have a watch, a reasonably heavy ring, a book, a purse, a jacket, even shoes, you should not feel weaponless. Anything that can be used as a projectile or distraction will buy you time to elude the challenger or move in. What makes it so is not the object but how you use your mind.

Many people have been whipped with their own gun because the attacker could feel that they were afraid to use it. They froze. The weapon is not an object but the use of the object coupled with your own spirit. If you are possessed by fear, no weapon will help you. If you have faith in the power of the warrior within, you are always better equipped than the person who is attempting to harm you.

You are determined to stop an assault. It is not the same thing as willfully becoming a target and throwing away your life. A living warrior is far more effective than a dead one in stopping an assault. There is an instinctive and intuitive protocol that operates to move you out of harm's way even as you run toward it. A Samurai was always willing to risk his life under the sword, but he did not just stand there and let himself be struck down. He would parry the blade, block and counter-strike. His energy was directed at striking down his adversary, but in the process he avoided the oncoming blade of his enemy without thinking.

Even though you have taken on a dangerous mission, you must maintain faith in the Original Mind at work in you. If there is a way, the way is already known. If there is a possibility of acting it out, you are already acting it out. Follow through.

Remember, there is a difference between figuring out what to do on the linear plane and taking action the Zen way. The Zen way has no steps in between. You are already there and the mission is accomplished. You will never know this path without faith, plus its companion, action. The Bible says, 'Faith without works (action) is dead.' Don't just sit there ... do something.

Watchfulness

In days of old, just a few feet of cold steel
weighing no more than an arm
took one life at a time.
It made a sound like whispering wind
then eerie silence gave way to the thud
of one body landing in the dirt.
If only the defender had concentrated harder,
if only his eyes were faster,
fast enough to see the flinching muscles which
    moved the sword,
if only he had moved one foot back,
if only ...

Today the cold steel weapon is many feet long –
we count its weight in tons.
It moves in miles per hour,
but the one who holds it in their hand is the one
who must be aware ...
this steel cuts many ways,
all unintended fall before it
when the eyes move from the path.
One instant can cost everything.
The road warrior cannot ignore anything,
the movement in the corner of the eye,
a flicker of light,
a sudden sound.

In days of old, the warrior and his sword
were one element sensing life,
avoiding death.
Today we take up steel in a different way.
But do we know we are nonetheless traveling the
   warrior's path,
where awareness, spontaneity and wisdom
can lead us safely home?
A road may look the same
but what is on the road,
who is on the road,
changes moment by moment.
The Samurai could not be careless facing one
   challenger,
but cold steel rushes on either side of you.
Staying alert, you avoid one encounter after
   another.

CHAPTER TWELVE

I HAVE NO ARMOR; I MAKE GOODWILL AND HONESTY MY ARMOR

There was a time when warriors layered themselves in thick leather or sheets of metal and chainmail to ward off blades of death. There was an expectation that someone would attempt to do them harm. In times of war, such an event was highly probable. While armor was not 100% foolproof it served to buy the warrior extra time to outmaneuver his assailant while he sought means of penetrating his protection.

If we come to rely too much on artificial armor of any kind then it will serve to work against us. The legendary Achilles thought he was protected but an arrow penetrated the one area of his body that was vulnerable ... his heel. For the archer there was only one target to aim for on Achilles, the one point that, when struck, would take his life. The true armor for Achilles would have been secrecy – no one should have known that he was vulnerable anywhere.

The fictional hero Superman is invulnerable to the extreme. Nothing can harm him ... normally. Yet even the 'man of steel' has his own Achilles Heel. It is called Kryptonite. These rocks flung from his dead planet weaken him to the point that he is weaker than a normal man. In that state, Superman can be beaten or killed. Like Achilles, his armor would be silence. No vulnerability should be revealed, to put the blade in the hands of the enemy. The purpose of armor is to keep the harmful from coming through. It does not have to be tangible to do its job.

Try loving people. Everyone was once someone's little baby boy or girl. Everyone falls back into innocence when they are asleep. So look for the good or likeable qualities in everyone you encounter or give them the benefit of the doubt. Once you start seeing the good in people you will naturally feel better around them. You will enter a building with a ready smile and discover that you can engage in brief conversation with anyone. You will touch people with your words, your disposition and perhaps, on occasion, you will offer them your hand.

What happens is that people will enjoy having you in their presence. You radiate a positive field to them. This is known as positive *ki* in Japan. It is something that people can feel, just as they can feel the opposite. When your *ki* is positive and strong, people simply like you. Since you are able to generate this field wherever you go you will make friends naturally as you come and go. Even if there was trouble, you may find that others intervene on your behalf.

Years ago I went to a nightclub that I knew was in 'white territory', according to the rules of the time. I did not believe in the validity of racism. A friend of mine was performing there. He wanted me to come but warned me of the danger. I went. I was no sooner in the door than five men approached me and began insulting me. I stood my ground. Moments later a man yelled out, telling them to leave me alone. He invited me to sit with him. The threat was over and no blows were struck.

'I like your style,' the man said. Perhaps, in this case, a real man admires another one. He admired my courage and he showed courage to come to my aid. Real armor is not metal or thick leather. It is not mail or any kind of outer garment. It comes forth like a force-field. It takes some work to get there, but it is certainly worth the practice, and you can practice anywhere.

Another virtue that will build your armor is honesty. Giving a person his wallet back or handing back an expensive phone to the woman who dropped it is honest, but this is not the kind of honesty being spoken about. For once in your life, look within your heart and soul and be honest with yourself. People have all kinds of ideas about you – many of these you have encouraged. We most often work hard to show our best to the public, even burying much of our truth from many who are close to us. Even that is not our concern.

This is not an attempt to get you to come clean on the 6 o'clock news or on a reality show. Being honest involves examining your own mind, your own heart and your deeds, admitting the flaws and contradictions to be found, without making excuses. This is a very important exercise. Lying to yourself about yourself hides the true you from yourself. Read that again.

'Except you come as a child, you will in no wise enter the Kingdom of Heaven.' When you were an infant you were transparent. Your mind was empty, spontaneous and free.

Your actions and what few thoughts you had were pure. By pure, I do not mean good as opposed to bad or evil. Your thoughts were pure because you did not qualify or justify them. You experienced them and allowed them to fade away without comment. During this period of your life there was no internal pressure brought about by thought, nor any outer versus inner, or life versus death. There were responses to stimuli, hearing of sounds, colors to see, and so your life proceeded each moment.

As a baby your wore armor naturally. Your body was the armor of *you*, the soul, for you had not yet fallen fully into the carnal or flesh-centered realm. Your mind was becoming your sword but it would not be long before outsiders, 'others', took control of the hilt. It is one thing to be educated about the world you live in so that you understand how it operates. It is another to be molded into a pawn within it. When mental training causes us to lose connection with our fundamental nature we have crashed into a pseudo-world. Our natural sword, our soul sword, is now nothing more than a shovel. This is so because we learn to lie to ourselves rather than allow our true nature to arise.

We may assume a role for a job or for a season but it is a tragedy when, in private, we make ourselves out to be what we are not. When we dam our mind with lies, the mind becomes a quagmire. It cannot flow. When we are honest with ourselves our mind flows like water … a subterranean current of great power. As a college student, I asked the famous author James Baldwin about extreme views. He spoke of a pendulum and how it swings from one side to the other until it comes to rest in the middle.

We do not need to grasp at lies or extreme views of

ourselves. We do not have to hold on to any view at all. Other people will draw their conclusions and typecast us to suit their ideas but we do not need to be party to their illusions, making them our delusions. It is far better that we let all such views, good and bad, fall through the sieve. We are neither this nor that. We can do this, we can do that, but we are not to classify ourselves in this way. It is not possible to be of one mindset all the time.

When we overly identify with one side and one view, we feel out of sorts when something else emerges in us. This is you, this is you, and this is you also. By allowing a variety of feelings and changes to flow through you without giving energy to them, you allow them to transform into a current that is pure energy, to be used as needed. Energy is comprised of multiple elements – it is not just one thing. When you say, 'I am a this,' your mind becomes an object or it must, by the law of agreement, conform to certain principles to comply.

Is a hand open or closed? Is your voice always soft or always loud? You prefer to walk but would you ever run? If for some reason your hand was closed, would it still be your hand? If your soft voice morphed into a booming tirade, would that really be you? All at once your cadence changes, and you sprint down the street. Would you deny that the person running down the sidewalk was you? Just who do you think you *are*? Herein lies the problem. *Who do we think we are?*

There are so many ways we block our mind. It is these thought-constructions which build the schematic we believe is our mind. Cattle travel along a narrow corral which eventually comes to an end at the slaughterhouse. We must not lock in on the 'thing-events' of our lives and turn them into definitions of who we are. Our mind is not a schematic.

When it is No-Mind your possibilities are endless. Traveling down the corral you realize the threat and veer off the given course to find safety. An elephant is held in check by a rope attached to a peg in the ground. It could pull away by exerting the slightest pressure but its mind believes that the peg is sufficient to stop it, so it goes no further. The elephant does not comprehend its strength, and neither do you.

If all your understanding comes from what you are told, you have been pegged. You are following parameters set by others. If you are going to practice honesty, recognize that you can never know yourself through feedback from others. You can never know yourself through data of any kind. In fact, the attempt to 'know' prevents the experience of *being*.

Zen teachings help. The mind expresses itself in three *nen*. The first *nen* is the undivided, unblocked action. The second *nen* reflects on the experience and the third *nen* expands on the second. You jump out of the way of a car without thinking. Then you recognize what you did. Finally, you may think, 'I could have been killed.'

If your mind is functioning freely, you will respond in Zen-like manner first. You will act. If your mind is blocked by many thoughts you may think, 'I am going to be killed.' You might freeze and be hit by the car. Holding oneself to a narrow image creates fear and promotes failure. You do not know what you are capable of. You move, you breathe, you have your being in God.

We could say that another way. Everything originated in emptiness, undefined. We tend to fear having no handles

111

to grab, but this fear is taught. We are self-contained. That which is essential to our being is present. We must allow it to mature as we live each day.

On the one hand, we are gracious and accepting of others. We send positive *ki*, goodwill to them, giving us virtuous energy. On the other hand, we extend this same gift to ourselves by allowing our mind to freely express itself. This free expression is something that is going on within you. That does not mean that you will carry out every thought or say everything which comes to your mind, but what you think, what goes on within your secret refuge, is your private domain. You will notice a new fluidity when your practice these things, a new excitement. Suddenly, there are more possibilities before you. Your armor is tailored just for you.

Protected

They say the world is cruel and the world is cold:
at all times I carry with me a friendly heart
and a warm smile ...
among strangers
I would be the one person
no one fears approaching.
When a chill in the air sends
a shiver through souls,
I am the one who enters with a smile
whose eye-contact
softens the glare.

I am protected but I have
no conventional weapon.
I just love people, each one,
I wish them well from my heart ...
and this is how I pass
through dangerous places,
seeing no danger
just potential friends in unlikely places.

Everywhere
I see reflections of what I myself also am,
coming and going
feeling up or feeling down –
there is nothing new.
I give myself away as I enter new places
so there is nothing to take,
I am shielded by a suit of armor
made of genuine love.
Only the most evil of spirits
would seek to break through that
and what he would find
makes me shudder at the thought
of what awaits him.

CHAPTER THIRTEEN

I HAVE NO FORTRESS; I MAKE MY IMMOVABLE MIND MY FORTRESS

As a young man I heard stories of one warrior fighting many warriors and defeating them all. This was especially true of the Samurai swordsman. It looked impossible. After my satori I discovered that defending myself against many attackers was easy. I was in a fortress and safe in the bosom of the Immovable Mind. My survival or wellbeing did not depend on great skill, a superior weapon or the arrival of the police to save the day. Immovable Mind was all I needed.

Somehow, everything arose from that state of mind, that presence. There are many kinds of fighters and numerous martial arts. Some are very impressive. It takes years of training and conditioning to do what some people are able to do. However, this is not your path. The others are doing a good job of whipping the cart into shape but you are training the horse. To use a traditional Zen metaphor, you are training the ox. The cart will go wherever the ox takes it.

Where do you feel safe? Are you safe in the mountains, in a brick building, in a locked car, surrounded by several of your toughest buddies? Is that what makes you safe? Well, you will not always have those conditions or those people with you. There is a deeper, more fulfilling way to feel safe. Take refuge within your mind. By that, I do not mean hide in your mind.

Hiding in your mind is a delusion akin to a child thinking it is invisible because its hands are covering its face. We assume that this thing we call mind is in our head, because we associate mind with the hardware, the brain. What I am speaking of, that which might be referred to as the Cosmic Mind, Buddha Mind or Divine Mind, is not in your head. It is the ocean in which our bodies, the Earth and the universe move. Take refuge within this. Permit yourself to feel the electric sensation of being enveloped in this protective power.

Taoists refer to the Tao as the 'mother of all things'. My teacher, Sadguru Sant Keshavadas, spoke of cosmic *Shakti Kundalini*, the Universal Mother. This feminine expression is at the same time nurturing, powerful and infinite. In the West we are accustomed to thinking of God, thus the highest possibility of our self lies in the masculine. Power is assumed to be a masculine trait, so aggression and forcefulness follow. The feminine, however, is yielding, receptive, embracing. Something happens when we acknowledge our feminine nature, when we allow it to engulf us. Once again your mother wraps you in her arms.

When you are a baby, you cry and your mother comforts you. She finds you where you are. Take refuge right here in the Universal Mother. You cannot find her until you recognize that she exists, until you give her love. Just this consciousness is your unconscious mind, No-Mind, working for you. Santji taught that we should pay our respects to this aspect of ourselves. In paying homage we give greater life to it by our very recognition. We acknowledge it, her, the Universal Mother, functioning as Mind, but we do not own or control her. We are students at her feet, just as we sat at the feet of our human mothers.

Our mother is always there to protect and guide her children, at any age. So it is with this Cosmic Mother. We attune ourselves to her voice and subtle guidance. In reaching out to the masculine side of the Godhead, to enter His presence we have only to recognize that He is real. It is not different with the Cosmic Mind or Cosmic Mother, which works with us in this material realm.

We must *believe*. The mere act of believing promotes experiences, and then our faith naturally grows. We are admonished to use Immovable Mind as our fortress because there are those who have found it to be a great refuge in times of trouble. Your self-flagellating ego-mind will never provide such shelter. Yet, there is a mountain that offers you protection against the storm. It is not within you – you are within it. Feel the sheltering arms of your Mother. She is your Mind.

There are some fighting arts which openly embrace the feminine nature – T'ai Ch'i, Aikido and various forms of Kung Fu. The Shaolin were Taoists and practiced a life of service. They displayed a gentle nature externally, but they had access to great power when they needed it.

To take shelter in the feminine way, the way of the Universal Mother, is to take shelter in mysterious power.

The mountain is immovable but those who move with force destroy themselves by rushing against it. Its immovability is its strength. This mind we speak of, cosmic in nature, mother-like in its essence, is immutable through all time. It is said of the Lord, 'He is the same yesterday, today and forever.' This Mind, original and unfathomable, does not change either. You can count on it because there is no place of ego in it.

Mother – the Immovable Mind

A sudden noise and trouble strikes.
I take shelter where there is none.
My body is wrapped in mighty wings
as tender as a mother's gaze ...

No matter how futile it looks,
there is no avenue to my vulnerable places.
I am secure in the loving ocean
that is the Eternal Mother,
the womb from which the universe came.

Standing motionless,
I feel the rising and falling of the cosmic breath.
I breathe it, I bow ...
In bowing I recognize that there is nothing
    to fear.
Already I am anchored in the great stillness,
immersed in eternity.
From where I am
the drama plays on ...
I watch calmly detached.
It is nothing more than television ...
this body is but a character
in the story.

CHAPTER FOURTEEN

I HAVE NO SWORD; I MAKE MY SURRENDERED EGO MY SWORD

Even though I live in this age I do not identity with guns. I served a short stint in the sheriff's office in my hometown of Portsmouth, Virginia. One time I was called to the colonel's office because I was carrying a collapsible police baton. Every officer has one, but at that time they had not been certified for law enforcement officials. The way I saw it, it was far better to hit a suspect than shoot him. I did not want to develop reliance on a gun to feel safe. I felt secure in my warrior skills.

My baton was not taken from me but I was told to carry it back home. Although I was trained in the use of a handgun I did not think of it as my primary weapon. One day, I intervened in a situation on the street when two men were chasing another man with chains in their hands. The two men with the chains were white and the one running was black. I told them to drop them, and they did. I asked them to tell me what was going on. Apparently, there had been some kind of altercation on the road and the black man hit one of the other men. At least, that was one story.

Everything changed when the black man picked up one of the chains and started toward the other men. 'Drop it!' I said, but he kept approaching them. I yelled out again. I had my hand on the butt of my gun as I moved in front of him. Blind to my presence, he swung the chain. I ducked under it and caught him under his right arm as I whirled, and threw him in an arc to the concrete. With my knee in his chest, I turned and asked a citizen to call for backup. I was off-duty and this was a little before cell phones.

People in the neighborhood, black people, were angry with me for subduing the suspect. I suppose they felt I should have just let him hit the men, because I am black also. The other two men had obeyed my command. The man on the ground did not. Even though he was swinging a heavy chain I felt no need to pull my gun. Everything was handled and I controlled the throw so that he was only startled, not hurt by the fall.

The Kamakura era Samurai came in contact with Zen and discovered a different dimension to the sword. Authentic Zen practice turned razor-sharp steel into a living object, endowed with wisdom and the power to move on its own. Actually, the source of this new sword arose from within the consciousness of the warrior himself. It was not the result of technical training or a new exercise program. Something spiritual occurred in the warrior. His own expanded vision and experience was expressed in his sword.

There is a natural relationship between the swordsman and Zen. The swordsman is alone before his adversary. In a moment, in the time it takes to recognize a flash of lightning, he could be cut down. His concentration must be strong, to screen out useless distractions. He must be flexible, to be able to move in any direction without attachment to any direction. He must be committed to going forward fearlessly into the unknown – resolute, no matter what. The swordsman must act immediately when opportunity presents itself. Above all the swordsman must be able to act from the unconscious. Thus, like Zen monks, the Kamukura Samurai were learning to renew their minds.

A Samurai once visited a Zen master. He told him he was about to embark on a journey to test his skills against the best warriors he could find. 'Why don't you start here?' the master said. The Samurai did not know what to make of the request.

'You are not a warrior. You don't use a sword.'

'This will do,' said the master, picking up a *hossu*, a horsetail fan. 'If I defeat you, you will stay and become a monk.' Now armed, the Zen master stood before the Samurai. The warrior attacked but felt the fan hit his face. That was the beginning and it was the end. Every time he moved he felt the sting of the fan. It was as if it was everywhere at once. At last, exhausted, he gave up.

The master signaled for his attendant to shave the warrior's head: now he would be a Zen student. In answer to the question of how he could defeat a seasoned warrior with nothing but a fan, the master revealed, 'The Zen mind sees into the functionality of all things.' The fan was his sword and he used it that way.

The ego causes us to take pride in what we know but the downside is that we feel inadequate when we face someone who may know more. The ego is a catch-all for our memories and experiences, and for years of feedback and opinions. It

121

is not the Original Mind. The ego is clearly in the box with a lid on to hold it in place.

It is not the Oceanic Mind, it is the puddle. A puddle is water, but you cannot sail a ship on it or swim in it. The puddle is not filled with life. You may ask the question, 'How can I deal with all of these unknowns? How do I know I can handle emergency situations or act appropriately when the time comes?' The answer is that you do not have the answers. The purpose of this book is to prove to you that the answers are there anyway, but just outside of the realm of cognition. You act, then you know. First *nen*, second *nen* ... ohhh!

We humans are linked to each other like computers on a network. We look different but we would not function as human beings without a basic commonality that was there from the beginning. Those who look at the world pragmatically see things one way, while those who are sensitive to its unseen nature experience it in another.

Scientists have kept records and passed down data that has permitted the growth of scientific knowledge. It is also true that those people who have been chosen to map the inward nature of humanity have also passed down their understanding, but in an entirely different way. Those who receive this 'spark' must trigger that spark in others. They are not scientists. They do not encourage long explanations. They are transmitting something that is real but, as Zen folk say, 'beyond sophistry'.

When it happens, you, what you do and how you act are forever transformed. The Samurai faced the Zen master but, on the other hand, he was really battling his ego. He thought he had to prove his greatness through matches.

He could become a genuine student only when he was willing to surrender his ego and give up his delusions.

A warrior prayed for insight into his discipline before the shrine of Lord Hanuman. As he walked away from the shrine, a monster leaped in front of him. His sword was instantly in his hand, and he slew the beast without so much as a single thought. His prayers had been answered. It is normal and expected that we act consciously and rationally to respond to various situations as they arise. Such responses lie within the realm of our control. This is not where the sword of no-sword comes from. The ego cannot seize hold of such an illustrious weapon.

Without understanding the possibilities that await you, you never reach further. When we fail to reach out, there is no chance of growth. The very first Zen story I read was about a professor of Buddhism who visited a Zen master. The professor talked on and on about what he knew of the subject. The Zen master offered him a cup of tea. He poured out the steaming liquid, but did not stop when the cup was full.

The professor spoke up, saying, 'The cup is overflowing.'

'Just like your mind. How can I teach you about Zen when you are already filled with so many ideas?' In the Zen way, less is more.

Sadguru Sant Keshavadas set an example for me. He never took personal credit for his talents or wisdom. He always credited God and downplayed himself. Yet I observed him as he wrote one book after another, recording many hours of music and speaking tirelessly about the Dharma. His energy seemed without end.

The power to write books, create music or express any

other creative endeavor is not different from the power being expressed in a warrior when the need arises. Our Original Mind, which is ego-less by nature, does not make distinctions between one activity and another. It is the ego which partitions off our energy-field into likes and dislikes. It establishes time and energy levels according to its selective designations.

Another great mentor of mine was martial arts master, C O Neal of Portsmouth, Virginia. Many times a martial arts champion and black belt honoree, Master Ronald Duncan came from his direct lineage. Master Neal was always smiling and kind. Though he was a police officer, he never demonstrated that attitude before his students. He was humble, yet he garnered great respect from people in the field.

Master Neal would often invite me home for dinner and we would spend hours discussing Bushido and trading moves. The more I yielded before him, the greater my understanding grew. After my satori I accepted Master Neal as the physical master I must pay homage to on the martial path. It is because of that relationship that the path to legitimate black belt rank opened.

I did not need this designation to defend myself, but Master Neal showed me that it would be a passport to teach other martial artists the Zen way. Though I already had an unexplainable insight and ability in the martial way I am known for, I had to step back so that Master Neal could prepare me to meet the rank and file. I laid my ego at his feet. I have never regretted it.

The sword is the symbol of my Soul Sword Zen Mission. Though it stands there with its blade gleaming against a blue-black field, I do not have the desire to cut people down. I can, but it is not my desire. It is not my meditation. It is taught that there are two swords: one kills and one saves. The soul sword preserves life. It is dedicated to protecting the original nature of what we are, against the backdrop of deceivers who want only to diminish our soul life on this planet.

The scriptures remind us that we are not fighting against flesh and blood but against spiritual wickedness in high places ... against principalities. As such, the forces are not easily discerned. The person who throws a rock into a crowd is the most likely to escape harm when the melée breaks out. The wise warrior is not of kill-mentality because he is aware that human beings are the pawns in a spiritual war.

Those who are not rooted mentally and spiritually can easily be pushed over the edge to do harm to themselves and others. Understanding this, the Zen Warrior stops the threat. This is *budo* by definition ... ending the struggle. The full force of his concentration is given to this task. However, should it become necessary, the sword that saves can transform into the sword that kills. If this happens, the aggressor will have slain himself for refusing to accept mercy. A malevolent force may perceive mercy as weakness and press the battle to a different conclusion.

I own several swords but I have no swords. I do not carry steel swords with me, hidden discretely under my coat. I was accused of that once, but it never happened. The truth is even more exciting. If you allow these teachings to sink in, you will not need to carry a sword or a gun to defend yourself when all else fails.

If you surrender your ego to the Inner Master, you will have a sword present the instant you need it. A sword is nothing but the elements forged to be an instrument in your service. It is at once a manifestation of mind and, at its best, a tool of your spirit. That means anything in the material world can be your sword – even your own body.

Remember, the sword which manifests only when your ego is surrendered does not draw its power from your own database of skills. It is not dependent on your conscious knowledge at all. When your ego is surrendered, your spirit uses the senses. It sees through the eyes, hears through the ears and acts according to its own nature which, though in this world, is not *of* it.

I had the opportunity, the blessing, to experience the protective power at work on an occasion when I was absolutely oblivious to danger. I was coming home about midnight one night, with my guitar on my shoulder. I was a teenager and it was summer. I suddenly grabbed the guitar and held it over my head. At that moment, a brick hit it and smashed through the wood. I realized immediately that I would have been dead were it not for that guitar.

The curious thing was this. Unlike the times when I received some warning, I had felt nothing – no sign of danger. In this case I had to conclude that I was guided by God, by Great Spirit. This was completely beyond my input or sensitivity. I just moved the guitar over my head and immediately felt a brick hit it. One fraction of a moment later, and I would have been dead.

When we reach out to the source of our being, recognizing that we come from the Spirit, we are able to establish two-way communications with Spirit. We may pray and otherwise chat on and on to God, but can we receive guidance direct from the Spirit into our spirit? In

that case, the young and receptive me, who was always
walking along talking to God as Father, was saved. My own
arms, my own guitar, became my sword and shield. You
have to reach to touch the higher experience.

Lightning Sword

I walk the dark streets
unarmed and unafraid –
if there is to be any fear
let others who would stop me fear.

This is my domain,
the only domain I know –
the grass is my carpet.
The night sky is the ceiling
of my majestic palace.

I walk on
smiling as I go.
I do not know all the faces of all I see
but I recognize the essence
of my Original Family.

There is a deceiver whom some say is mighty.
I hear he seeks to cut me down.
He draws courage, learning that I have no
    weapons,
but eyes can see and hands can grasp.

I sit in meditation, I walk in meditation,
I lie down and get up in meditation.
If the enemy leaps out of nowhere,
so will my lightning sword.

There will be three flashes of lightning
as it cuts through
the body
the mind
and the soul ...
but he will never see a thing.
I walk the streets unafraid,
My sword is with me ...
always ready.

CHAPTER FIFTEEN

I HAVE NO MAGIC; I MAKE SUBMISSION TO DIVINE WILL MY MAGIC

Sant Keshavadas taught me that if I surrendered to Divine Will, God would make the most extraordinary things happen to authenticate my mission. If you surrender, you may suddenly find your life becoming magical. You will not make people disappear or saw a lady in half – these are illusions – but the universe, the Earth itself abounds with magic so subtle, so marvelous, that most people fail to see it. Learning to recognize that magic is a part of your warrior training. It will boost your faith, recharge your spirit and help you to participate more fully in the master plan for humankind.

The first step is locking in on Divine Will. Just what is Divine Will and how do we sign up? Do we *want* to sign up? Is Divine Will user-friendly? We will explore these questions, but first we must examine the topic closer. Divine Will presupposes there is indeed a Divine Presence. The signature of my e-mail reads, 'The only proof I ever needed that God exists … is that I am.' That sums it up completely for me.

Many people engage in wordy discourse and argue scripture to establish their reasons. The question is personal, involving the active participation of your spirit over the intellect. Long ago I realized that, when it comes to the Divine, I throw up my hands in the universal symbol of no-contest. The only unbelievable aspect of all this to me is that such marvelously complex beings as human beings could ever doubt that they are indebted for their existence to someone even more marvelous.

As a writer I can only imagine my characters arguing among themselves as to whether I, their creator, am real or imaginary. If you believe in the Divine, you have to ask if you are willing to let the Divine take charge. Your carefully thought-out plans will be of no use to you once you enter that union.

Divine Will works with Divine Vision. Human beings have a narrow view of life and the world, but the Divine is concerned with the whole of creation – after all, every part of it is like a cell of its own being. When you enter into His Will, you may find that you are serving a larger, grander vision than the one which pushes you alone to the top. By submitting to Divine Will you become a knight on the cosmic chessboard. He will use you as He wills.

Many people expect a type of genie they can control and bend to their will. This most certainly is not the highest view. The Divine is the Master in this relationship, but there are benefits. For one, when you yield to Divine Will your *ki* or *ch'i* is the strongest possible, because you have become a vessel of the supreme Spirit. Such a change cannot go unnoticed. Since there are so few who enter into this symbiotic relationship, you are protected and supported because you, as a conscious and willing manifestation, are *needed*.

There are different kinds of warriors. I am sure you know that. In addition to the kind whose job it is to fight or kill for their countries, there are warriors of the Spirit. A warrior of the Spirit, to truly be so, must be a person who submits to Divine Will. Those who act solely under a religious banner may not qualify. Most people of that kind are following a human leader who is interpreting teachings for them. They are working out agreements in their head. This is not the path of the spiritual warrior. The spiritual warrior can only be led by Spirit. No outside interpretation or human pressure can override the authority within. The spiritual warrior is a soldier of humanity because that overall vision and compassion drives him as it does his Lord.

Consider Gandhi. He was an attorney by education but he did not practice law in the traditional sense. He gave up worldly possessions, strapped on a loincloth and served his people, fighting for their independence from Britain. He believed in peace. He practiced peace to the extreme. When he was assassinated he put his palms together and said one word, 'Ram'. That was one of the Hindu names for the Lord. If Gandhi wanted to live from his own ego, he had plenty of opportunities, but instead he stayed rooted in a higher will. His people did win their freedom and he lives on in spirit and mind, still serving humanity.

Joan of Arc always fascinates me. When I read her story in school I could not comprehend how a young woman could be burned alive in the fire and not cry out. She believed she was on a divine mission. The Maid of Orleans led her army through victorious campaigns, but there were those who thought her victory was of the devil. Had she screamed in agony it would have been a victory for her detractors, proof that the devil was her friend. Instead, the silent maiden became a legend.

Years later, I witnessed a newsreel of a Buddhist monk sitting in the midst of flames. He did not cry out. In church I learned about three Hebrew boys who were also thrown into an inferno – they did not scream but neither did they burn. They were on a mission for God. Any normal person can be forgiven for agonizing when on fire. The fact that a person does not respond to great suffering brings attention to their case. A person surrendered to the Divine Will is immersed in the Divine. In a moment like that, such a person is wrapped in the wings of love. The body may burn but the integrity of the Spirit is kept intact. The *Bhagavad-Gita* sings of the immortal soul, 'Fire can not burn it ...'

Here's another thing I learned from my guru. We cannot do anything extraordinary by ourselves. It may sound gracious to refuse to take credit for great acts, but it is simply the truth. The more you learn about the inner nature of your being, the more you realize that we give ourselves too much credit. You may be endowed with great intelligence but you did not produce the brain you possess nor the body which carries it.

How far can you go back in your memory? Can you remember the day you were born? Probably not. At one point in time and space there was no you, as you know yourself today. Your bodily form did not exist, with its liberal sharing of DNA from your ancestors, and there was no memory of anything to do with Earth, life or the universe. There was a moment in time in which you were just empty space – and by that I do not imply stars and planets. There was nothing to see and no you to be aware of it. *So exactly what did you do to get here?* Please meditate on that for a moment before going on.

Satori reveals the answers to such questions in the same way as eating food reveals its taste. When you no longer have to justify or explain your existence, when you cast aside feeble attempts to reconstruct life after the fact, something happens to your head, rather akin to letting the air out of a balloon. Reality reveals itself to you alone.

I use the word *satori* because it is the word I first learned to describe what happened to me. Nothing in the English language pointed to it and other languages offered alternatives that were more difficult to say. People have had this direct experience and never knew a word for it ... and they did not need a word unless they were doing as I am doing. The word points to it, but you must look for yourself. Traditionally, Zen as taught by Buddhists is non-theistic. That is not an indication that Zen is non-theistic. I came from a Christian background, so the challenge to me is to approach this direct path in a way that God-centered believers can sense.

There are levels of faith. The deepest expression of faith does not wrap itself in formality, but it is what can transform an individual. If you are going to sense the Divine Will you must do so *for you*. I see the Zen approach to be that of a prodigal son or daughter bent on returning to the Father. Big brother has already told you that Father wants you home. Now he is gone because he knows you know the way. For each son or daughter there is a personal key. Once you use that key the journey begins. It is just you and the Father.

The Kingdom of Heaven, where the Father dwells in His secret place, does not open to flesh and blood. So before you can make progress you have to leave certain things behind.

> A cow jumped through a window –
> its big head, horns,
> its entire body and hooves went through,
> but the tail did not make it through.

We see things backwards. We are born of the Eternal in an impermanent form. Even though we pay homage to God, who is Spirit, we tend to focus mostly on the flesh-centered or carnal life. The carnal perspective blinds us as to our true estate and the real nature of our current conditions. When we strip away the false we experience change.

Only the real can return through the portal, back to the bosom of the Father. I use the word 'Father' because that image is warm and fuzzy to our human memory. However, this Father is our sire in the universal sense, the one who cannot be embraced by the body. Union with this Father is more like a river flowing into the ocean, becoming one consciousness. Jesus spoke of this: 'I and the Father are one. I would that ye become one, as we are one.'

Since the conflict of the mind is duality, 'a double-mind is unstable in all its ways.' Healing that split is an all-important mission. This is what we work on in Zen practice.

Christ said, 'Not my will but Thy Will be done.' In this way, Jesus solved the problem of duality. He agreed to follow the Will of God, not his own. By taking that path the actions of Christ truly are the actions of God on Earth. No matter how difficult, he followed the path laid out for him.

What prince and heir to the throne would leave a beautiful wife and child and a wealthy kingdom to become a beggar in rags? Over 2,500 years ago, Siddhartha Gautama, better known as the Buddha, did just that in search of an end to suffering. Given all his choices, he chose an uncertain spiritual quest over a safe life of luxury and power.

Just because you seek or embrace the Divine Will, it does not mean you will have to quit your job or sacrifice your life. What it does mean is that you will be open to a higher dimension of life, full of joy and peace and, because of that, you will also be open to expanded sensitivity. Your compassion will grow and you will seek to be of service to others. What is more, you will have just what you need when the time comes. You will also know what to say in every circumstance presented to you. You will be able to do things and you will know things because your mind becomes merged in that divine consciousness. You will speak from that wisdom-pool.

Sadguru Sant Keshavadas was scheduled to speak at an ashram in Richmond, Virginia. I, along with other members of the Norfolk ashram, went with him. When he was called to speak, the sadguru said, 'The great American yogi, Kitabu, will speak.' He did not tell me he was going to do this. I rose from my seat and spoke. I do not remember anything of what I said.

I do remember Indian devotees following me around afterwards to find out who I was and how it was that Santji chose me. 'We have the same teacher,' I said. 'The Holy Spirit.' That was the answer given to me. It silenced everyone. In fact, when I finished talking, Santji punctuated the ending by saying, 'The Holy Spirit has spoken.'

When you surrender yourself to Divine Will you function in overdrive. It is the difference between using a computer offline and online. Surrendering to the Divine Will may sound scary but it is the most natural thing in the world. In the beginning of time, the mind of man was naturally attuned to the Divine. There was no other mind. When body was fashioned it was infused with both spirit and mind. Where could they come from?

Original Man did not have to second-guess himself, acting with hesitation or fear in his thought-life. Oneness is undivided, and undivided was his mind as it functioned day by day. Only when he was challenged to question his perfection, and when he made the unnecessary step to improve on his consciousness, did he achieve the opposite. He threw his mind into turmoil, creating a war within himself.

A child possesses parts of his or her mother and parts of the father. These differences blend to create a person who often manages to favor both parents while remaining a unique individual. Man is born of Heaven and Earth. It is the Heaven part that has been forgotten, although people attempt to graft on the heavenly idea through conscious effort. This may make people feel good but it is not what is needed to restore the original relationship of oneness.

The pollution of the mind started with an idea injected by an alien spirit, that is, by one who stood outside the symbiotic circle. Original Man was made out of God and Earth, so they fit together. The outsider, the adversary, was a renegade who operated freely from his own dimension. He had his own plan. He knew what it would take to undermine man's spiritual roots and he made a direct assault on man's mind. The moment man's mind turned on itself, his spiritual nature was corrupted. It is easy to see how important the mind is to the restoration of man to his proper place.

You should expect something extraordinary to happen. When you surrender to Divine Will you are opening the dam to a higher dimension. This power is benevolent, the author of creation. With no words spoken and none heard, your understanding expands along with your sense of loving and being loved.

Surrender brings with it the need for humility. Allow the change to take place in you but remember this is not something happening because of you. This is in the nature of things. You are clearing ego-space, and as you do so your awareness of *what is so* grows. You may recognize something for the first time. You may think you are the only person in the universe to have the experience. It is so. It is not so.

It is written that when one becomes enlightened, one meets all the Buddhas, past, present and future, face to face. Since there is only one True Mind, anyone who attains it understands the same things as the ones who came before or who come after. Whatever you see belongs to humanity. The only thing to do is to be grateful.

We have spoken about spiritual warriorhood and soldiers of humanity. The more you yield, the more you discover what is possible. I can strike a person down with a gentle touch of my finger but I also discovered that this same unexplainable power can heal or perform other miraculous deeds, without fanfare.

Perhaps one of the more amazing events from the scientific point of view was when I was called to the bedside of missionary Rosalee Barnes. She was in a coma, and the family was about to authorize the pulling of the plug. The next day was Mother's Day and the two daughters had not spoken to her since she fell into a coma over a week before. Her minister was there praying, as were others, including my sister Raheema who also knew her. I asked everyone to leave but my sister stood by. I then placed my hand on Rosa's forehead and told her to wake up. Within five minutes she came out of her coma and spoke in a loud, clear voice. I whispered to her and kissed her. As I left, I told the family that it was just a visit. She chatted with over 25 of her kinfolk. Five hours later she entered the final sleep. When I first heard the minister praying for missionary Barnes, I knew I could do something.

Rosalee believed in me, and that was a prerequisite to exercising faith. On an earlier occasion when I went to see her I heard someone screaming in pain. When I got to her room I saw that it was she. Another missionary was trying to comfort her. Without a word I took her in my arms and held her. She immediately fell into a painless sleep and I put her to bed. There is no how in these matters, only doing.

One of my students called to tell me goodbye. I asked where she was going. 'I am in the hospital and the doctors say I'm going to die,' she said.

'You're not going anywhere,' I said.

Five doctors had confirmed the medical diagnosis. Yet that very day she was released from the hospital because they could find no trace of the problem when they examined her again. I have found that, as you surrender, you gain authority. It is important to accept and act upon that authority. It is like being the deputy to a sheriff: you are not the sheriff but you can act on his behalf. If you do not accept this transference of power, your words will lack conviction – people will ignore you. By yielding to the Divine Will you become deputized. The power is proven in action.

I often go to court to stand for my students. When it is called for, I speak on their behalf. While I always give the judge respect, I do not speak to him with deference. I make it clear that I have authority and that I stand in that place even before him. This is conveyed by the manner in which I speak, the tone of my voice, my bearing. So far, I have never lost a single case. I understand that there are dimensions of power. For too long the governments of this world have controlled our minds. We must pay homage to the true power in the universe in order to provide Him with a channel in which to operate.

Remember, man's mind-splitting decision effectively locked God out of our universe. We must invite Him back. If we attempt this through church we keep the separation strong – He is there in Heaven and we are here on Earth. However, if we enter through the private door, we merge with Him. He sees through our eyes and tastes with our tongue. This is true union ... being one. If you *try* to do magic, it will be an illusion, no matter how mystifying it may be. However, if you permit Divine Will to take root in you, the magic will be real. Only the Divine really does magic. Presto! A planet teeming with life.

Magic Power

In and of himself,
he was not known for strength or courage.
In school he was the one always running
from those bigger, those who traveled in packs.
He longed for a magic power,
a wand to wave,
anything that would shield him
from the taunts, the blows, the looks of disgust.
He longed for power, for something magical to
    save him,
anything to turn his mind away from its
    tremors ...

One day a wise and strong man took him as a
    student.
Upon his chest was a star of radiant light.
The young one felt a current passing through him
    when he touched it.
'I deputize you,' said the wise man when training
    was done,
and the young man suddenly felt the power of
    The State acting through him.
He felt the authority of The State speaking
    through him when he moved his lips.
He now wore the star of authority,
though he had no power of his own, really.
He stood for the power,
and none of those who once came against him
dared do so again,

because this time the boy with no magic power
let power flow through him.
The True Warrior is like that, possessing nothing
    but reflecting all,
The mirror surrenders its surface.
The mirror is a jewel.

CHAPTER SIXTEEN

I HAVE NO MIRACLES; I MAKE THE DHARMA MY MIRACLE

An enlightened man once said, 'What miracle this ... I draw water, I carry fuel.'

A young woman experienced enlightenment when the bottom fell out of a bucket of water she was carrying. 'No more water in the bucket, no more moon in the water.'

Bodhidharma, the 28th Patriarch of the Buddha, faced a determined warrior who was so desperate to be his student that he cut off his arm and stood all night outside in a snowstorm. Moved by his determination, Bodhidharma asked what the man was seeking.

'To pacify my mind,' was his reply.

'Bring your mind out to me and I will pacify it.'

'No matter how hard I search I cannot find my mind,' said the aspiring student.

Bodhidharma replied, 'Then I have pacified your mind.'

What miracle this? Nothing done and yet everything is changed.

In another case a monk of a different Buddhist sect challenged a Zen master by saying that his master could stand on the opposite shore of a river bank and write on a tablet being held up by an attendant on this shore. The master's response was, 'Your fox may be able to do such tricks but that is not the purpose of Zen.'

There are many kinds of miracles. Those that are touted in religious teachings are of the supernatural order. There are certain fixed expectations we consider laws of nature, and when events occur that defy those laws we call them 'miracles'. When Jesus Christ broke a small portion of bread and fish in two and fed 5,000 hungry people, it was something that could not be explained by natural law.

When all hope seemed gone and the Hebrew children were being pursued to the sea by Pharaoh's army, Moses did as he was instructed by God, by Divine Will: he raised his staff and the sea rose up from its bed, creating an avenue of escape. Moses did not part the Red Sea, he simply raised his staff ... and right there is the proper Zen attitude. That is the miracle. Do I mean parting the Red Sea? No. The miracle, your miracle, would be in raising your staff with full authority.

When you understand your true nature you move in accord with it. Religions speak of miracles to boost the faith of believers. Miracles may be needed by some believers. However, Jesus himself did not base his mission on miracles alone. It was not his purpose to heal everyone, restore the lives of the fallen and feed the multitude each day. Miracles were attention-getters, while he was pointing to a higher kingdom. That kingdom was the source of miracles. The kingdom Jesus pointed to was the Kingdom of God, a supernatural kingdom if ever there was one. The operating system of that kingdom cannot be compared to the way of the world. Jesus performed big budget miracles. While it is not impossible, it is not likely that many will come who can duplicate the miracles he did.

On the other hand, there is another kind of miracle. These miracles are brought to you by Dharma. For the sake of clarity we can say that Dharma is that teaching which has the sole purpose of awakening your mind. Dharma is said to be transmitted from one mind to another – more accurately, from the Mind to the mind.

The term 'transmitted' is misleading. Let me illustrate. You are a child, and you have no idea that you have internal organs. An older boy tells you that you do have parts inside but you do not believe him. In frustration he hits you in the stomach. Moments later you have a stomach ache. You feel that organ standing out for the first time. The older boy has just 'transmitted' stomach to you but it did not leave him and appear in you. He made you aware, and mind received its presence as a truth. Dharma cuts through deceptions, breaks the bonds of illusion, freeing mind from its trap.

You are already party to many miracles day by day, moment by moment, but without opened eyes we take what we see and feel as the norm – we lose the excitement we once had just being alive. What has changed? We are given a linear education which, by design, limits our focus to a narrow track. We can spend so much time preparing to make a living that we do not *live*. We grasp concepts and forms because we have been taught to do that. Even our spiritual life must fit into a well-crafted box agreed to by the masses.

Believing has become a form of election-time politics: those who proclaim themselves to be lovers of peace and humanity spend much of their time attacking the belief systems of others rather than living out their own. Dharma is a two-edged sword that cuts through the one who uses it. It transforms the user.

The Dharma sword slices through your ego to restore the innocence of the No-Mind state you received directly from your parents when you were born. Yet this time, it connects with your life-experience, spontaneously generating instinctive wisdom, *prajna*. There is no space anywhere that is not miraculous. You yourself are a miracle, the way you move, the way you breathe, the way you respond.

The Dharma sword of the master penetrates your ego-mind to break down all the places where delusions hide. This very self you have built your life around is false. It amounts to owning an enormous house and living in only one room. You will not have the sense of being in a mansion if you do not go beyond the one room.

A person was speaking rather vainly about a religious experience. She spoke of her higher life. In the higher life she described, which took place before her current life, she saw herself appearing as the same person. However, our current appearance is the result of attributes transmitted through the DNA of our parents and ancestors. They do not reflect our primordial existence, which does not depend on DNA.

Do angels have DNA? The aspect of our being accessible only by ascension is of an angelic nature, Unborn. There is no more to be said about it. When we focus on our appearance, we hone in on the ancestral lineage rooted in the history of the material and linear world. This is the world where everything connects in some way. This is the world where Dharma is needed.

The student of Dharma has a tool that will one day free

his consciousness to bridge the dimensions of his being, permitting him to access the wisdom he needs to move through the everyday world. The world is three-dimensional. Man is a multidimensional being, but that does not mean you are aware of those other dimensions of self. It is popular today to speak about extraordinary adventures taking place through astral travel, remote viewing and the like, but this is not what we should be seeking. These are asides.

Powers, *siddhis*, naturally result from concentration enhanced by such disciplines as meditation but, from the very beginning, Sant Keshavadas told me that any such side-trips were a distraction from the highest attainment. Certain powers may appear, but the wise student ignores them and moves on. You are on an important journey. Do not stop to pick the flowers.

Samadhi is great concentration. Great concentration is a wonderful gift to have, but it can be dangerous also. One time, I sat in a donut shop and held a cup of coffee for eight hours without drinking a sip of it. I brought it to my lips. For me, only a moment had passed, but for the management it was eight hours. They called the police. While no harm was done, I had been completely oblivious to the passage of time. During that period I had no apparent existence.

Philip Kapleau Roshi, author of *The Three Pillars of Zen*, told the story of how he witnessed a Zen Buddhist go into meditation during an air raid in London. The man appeared so calm and serene, he stayed at the restaurant table with him rather than run for shelter. That was also samadhi.

The question I would ask is, *where are you living?* You are responsible for taking care of home base. If you live on planet Earth, your focus, your creative skills, your spiritual genius should be focused here. The Dharma is a medicine for the broken mind. The Dharma sword, to borrow a Zen phrase, 'cuts duality in twain'. The miracle of the Dharma is not that it takes you out of the world – it brings the world into clear focus. With realization you find yourself already at home.

The story of the Garden of Eden puts man center-stage in Creation. No scripture is of any importance unless you first accept it on faith, and second put yourself in the script. You were at center-stage of the Creation. When you lost autonomy of mind, you lost control of yourself and your world. You fell out of grace with your Creator because you were no longer like your Creator. You became a shadow of your real self.

What was broken? How is it fixed? Dharma is not a book. Dharma is not available as a software download. Dharma does not exist so as to be pinned down. In essence, Dharma itself is the spirit of the real Mind, the one that was working perfectly when you opened your eyes in the Garden that very first day. Dharma gets you past the double-edged flaming sword. Who would dare challenge an angel wielding such a weapon? Well, his sword cuts through flesh-centered beings. Do not enter that way. When you are of No-Mind, there is nothing to strike. When you are of No-Mind you belong in the Garden.

You know next to nothing about Heaven but people love to fantasize about their life there. What about Earth? The Garden of Eden is right here, and right here is but a run-down, low-rent district of the Garden. It would seem that our spirit is invested in regaining our proper state of mind and winning back what we lost. Talk about games ... wouldn't that be the greatest game of all?

Our adversaries learned an important game of warfare in the beginning. It worked then and it still works. Misdirect the mind of your intended victim and he will defeat himself from then on. The Bible tells us that the Adversary (the devil) suggested that man did not know right from wrong, and that learning that distinction would be a virtue. God did not want man to have that knowledge. The moment he fell for the trick, man's perception of himself changed, he feared God and the problems grew. Obviously, learning about good and evil was not virtuous. Zen saying: 'The conflict between good and evil is a disease of the mind.'

From the most ancient of days this diagnosis has been laid out. The disease of the mind is the internecine battle between good and evil. It is not a battle determining which side should be followed – it is far worse than that. In Genesis, God says, 'My spirit will not always stride with man because his deeds are evil.' The deeds of man are considered evil by God. He did not say that *some* deeds are evil. The statement suggests a plural view: 'Your deeds are evil.'

If we examine these words against the earlier Zen statement, 'The conflict between good and evil is the disease of the mind,' a glimmer of understanding emerges. As everything that appears before a cracked mirror will include the crack, everything that comes out of a diseased mind is, by definition, diseased. Since the Fall began with a mental decision, could it be that God is saying that the activities originating from this diminished mind are evil, as a matter of course? The new creature born out of the schism in man's mind is not God's Original Man. The activity of this creature cannot please him. That would be the trick of the Adversary, to defeat man by turning his own mind against him. By falling for this single ruse we lost our center. Most of us have searched in vain for a clue to its restoration.

If you can understand and apply these principles, you never need to worry about a masked man jumping out of the bushes. The true nature of warriorhood transcends the need for any weapon of steel because warfare is always being initiated at the spiritual level first. Something else has moved long before the fist clenches.

What has become our ordinary mind has been redirected in such a way as to make objects of thought. Thoughts have a pseudo-life. A hypnotist can cause some people to see whatever he projects and bend their will to his. Dharma cancels the power by revealing the Mind, not dependent on thought, images or an objectified mind. This is a great miracle. Without being encumbered by an objectified mind, we see the world *as it is*. We can respond to situations as they develop. This is the miracle we need to thrive in an ever-changing and increasingly violent world.

When your mind is free, it instantly recognizes red even before the word is called up in your mind. In the same manner, danger is recognized and responded to before the emergence of thoughts which bring fear. You simply *act*. Wisdom is inherent because wisdom emanates from nowhere in particular. When your mind is in a place of rest, wisdom emanates from you. It moves you. There is no separation.

Long ago, when I was just beginning this path of study, I read that a warrior who meditated was superior to one who had many martial techniques. I have since learned through my own practice that a person, not necessarily a warrior or martial artist, could excel in the area of self-defense with no learned techniques at all, if he or she embraces the principles of self-defense. In other words, they would only need to understand the objective – the means are already present within them. I have spent many years demonstrating and teaching this to experts and novices alike. Before the first move, you have won or lost the battle with your mind.

Faced with overwhelming odds, learn to rely on Dharma, and *there* is your miracle. The moment you opened this book you entered the Dharma realm.

No Miracles Here

How wondrous and marvelous!
The heroes of film
fly through the air,
somersaulting out of danger,
landing perfectly without looking,
faced with a multitude,
they do so with attitude.
One by one, group by group
the foe fall at the feet of the master.
His weapon never misses –
it returns as if by magic.
Who can compete,
who can defeat,
such a one as this?

Here though,
in the world in front of the screen,
in this real world,
I am empowered.
My hands move at my command,
my feet go where I desire,
nothing more than this I need
to recognize a miracle …
mind over matter.
As long as I keep my mind over my matter,
nothing else matters.

CHAPTER SEVENTEEN

ZEN WARRIORHOOD
IS A STATE OF MIND

You can have the most powerful and expensive car in the world, but if it does not have a working steering wheel it is not going to take you where you want to go. The exploration of the Bushido Code is vitally important, because the steering wheel of your body is your mind. In fact, that wheel decides the course of your life. Thus the importance of changing the way you think about the subject and yourself.

A warrior is a type of personality, but the words need not define the whole of the person. When we take a higher view, we cultivate the nature of the warrior. That way, it arises when needed. Where is the chef in you when you are not cooking, not thinking about food? You need not fear. When you enter the kitchen the chef is there. At the moment of need, the proper nature should arise, do the job and fade away.

We do not have to hold that image in our mind constantly. When we do that, we become an actor. Part of the time our attitude is not real – it does not fit the situation we are in. We practice to raise our consciousness and embrace the principle, then when we get it we must let it sink into the background, the unconscious.

It would not be realistic to say you could get a black belt in thirty days, because when we are learning a system by rote, we are locked into a pattern of teaching and learning that has been laid out over a course of time. The Zen Way is different. You have this moment and only this moment in which to live or die, to act or fail to act.

> Under the sword held high is hell making you
>   tremble,
> but go ahead,
> for there's the land of bliss.

If you apply yourself, if you get excited about these mental and spiritual workouts, you will advance. Your activity level will prove the point. When you get up from your chair, you will notice a difference in the way you walk. That will be your first sign that something is happening.

You can see what other people are doing. You can observe with your eyes their outward progress, but really you know nothing. You witness only physiological changes and they do not go deep enough. On the other hand, you will know immediately if you move faster, if you are more alert, and if you find that you are able to make appropriate decisions instantly when needed. When your sword moves as a flash of lightning, you notice. Thunder follows. So the interior work is the foundation of our approach, but all of it comes together.

CHAPTER EIGHTEEN

THE GAMER/WARRIOR: UNDERSTAND YOUR MISSION

Too often we spend great amounts of energy trying to understand the game or the mission, but we forget the most important element: we need to have a clear understanding of what we are doing. What is our role in the Great Game? The question can be explored another way: what is our function as an individual? The true answer to this question will not be found in the manual, the mission Bible. The true answer is user- and situation-specific. It applies *only* to the person who breathes in your space.

The question cannot be answered intellectually – that is not sufficient. The answer must be probed like a Zen *koan*, an enlightening question which cannot be logically answered – it must be probed with vital energy until there is an electrical overload in the brain itself, forcing the bio-computer to shut down and reboot. This satori experience is a fresh and hitherto unknown program that works in the background. There is no answer to speak of. The Gamer/Warrior's performance and responses form the answer.

To be satisfied with memorizing the rules and techniques of the game, of warfare or of unexpected encounters, is to be trapped in a dualistic scenario which first plays out within. That scene is then externalized. Vital seconds are lost when the brain believes it must monitor and sort out solutions in a linear manner. There is no substitute for decisive action. Great speed does not mean proper response. Understanding the mission is one thing, then there is programming your brain to serve that mission without hesitation.

The intelligence-field which includes the Cosmic Mind permeates all existence. It expresses itself according to the nature of the form it uses. It is said that 'fish swim to and from the air and birds fly back and forth through the air'. That statement is an observation of the mind at work in various life-forms. While it is true that the One Mind is universal, its uses are infinite and each type of life-form uses it in its own way. Only human beings have the power to direct its use according to their will.

Elephants do not fly. In centuries, elephants, as far as it is known, have not only made no progress in learning ways to take flight but they have made no effort to do so. By contrast, human beings could not fly either but, unlike the elephant, human beings sought the means to do so. In relatively short order we were sailing through the air with a window seat. The mind found a way to transport the body though the air with hand-crafted wings. In that case flight was the mission. The mission was clearly understood before it could be completed.

When I was flying at night surrounded by perhaps 200 people watching movies and listening to music, I realized that I was experiencing something mysterious. These things have not always happened. From the fabric, the elements, which have always been on the Earth, we keep fashioning something new and marvelous.

Here is another question to ponder. *Who or what made the plane?* Who or what conceived of the cell phone or the two-sided tape? You may be a master of trivia and can put the name of a person to each part of the question: I would say that you are wrong. The source is always the same, but the host, the agent, can be anyone.

One of my students, Leonard, designed a stylish shirt from the basic design of a pullover. His fellow students joined with me in urging him to pursue the design, but Leonard is an executive in another field. One night he came to our martial arts session wearing a beautiful version of his design. I complimented him. 'Oh, I bought this, Roshi. I've been seeing them all over the place.'

This revelation triggered good-natured laughter because we all knew that the design was originally his. Leonard would take his raw material to a seamstress to finish for him. His mission was a finished product, but he stopped there. The design needed to get out. It was still in the air to be picked up by another host. Probably no one stole the design, it just came to them one night.

If you think of yourself as the body, then it follows that an idea is personal property that cannot escape but, in truth, that is not the case. The One Mind has many bodies or hosts. If an octopus is reaching for something and, for some reason, a particular tentacle is not working properly, it can move another. If we recognize that intelligence is global or universal, we will see that you or I, as a single ego in that vast intelligence, have only a limited opportunity to make it our own.

In a sense this is an exciting feature in the Game of Life, the X-game. So one side of this business of One Mind is that we can receive at the unconscious level. The other side is that we can also make conscious use of it. We can say, 'Someone should invent a better ...', thus putting the request out there for someone to respond to, or we can say, 'I am inventing a better ...' Once you understand what you need to do, you understand your mission.

It is so important to realize who you are. It all depends on you. The space you occupy is occupied by no one else. You can only render service to humankind or advance spiritually while you are whole, alive. There is only a limited time on the clock, and the body has built-in obsolescence as it is. You must keep it in play.

Basketball is a team sport but each player knows that the score is determined by the number of baskets gained. It is to the advantage of each of the players to assist in achieving a basket, even if he or she is not the one who takes the final shot. The players must work in harmony, one in body, one in mind and one in spirit. Suppose the players did not understand the mission. If every player wanted to take the ball to the basket even when he was in no position to shoot, or failed to protect the shooter because he was jealous of his position, the result would be regular losses for the team. When you understand your role you can master it. The moment you accept your position, drink it up – the genius of that One Mind becomes the player.

It is more fluid than water. It is more like air, but it is empty of anything that is describable, yet it contains everything ... even you. This essential nature of our being, this Mind/No-Mind, is writing these words as me, while reading them as you. It is all there, but you have to point it in a direction.

Sadguru Sant Keshavadas told a story of a man who went to market and watched a demonstration of an amazing demon that could accomplish any task. The asking price was very cheap. After the man purchased the demon the buyer gave him instructions: 'Just keep him busy. If you fail to do this he will consume you.' That demon did not seem so attractive a purchase then.

The man put the demon to work right away. It did not take him long to realize that he was in trouble. He ordered the demon to build him a house. In moments, it was completed. He found another job, and that too was finished in moments. The man knew he was in trouble, so he asked his guru for advice. When he turned back to the demon, he said: 'Build a flagpole and go up and down it until I ask for you again.' The demon went up the pole, down the pole and up the pole countless times. After a while he was so tired it was a pitiful sight. He pleaded with his master to free him from the task. The master saw his opportunity. He told the demon that he could stop if he ended the contract between them. The demon agreed.

This demon is your mind. It can do anything but, if you give it nothing to do, it turns on you and consumes you in one way or another. The pole is a discipline, meditation, mantra, prayer, worship – those are spiritual disciplines. The discipline could be an artistic practice, music, dance, painting, martial arts or a craft. It could be your dedication to a particular form of work. You could focus on being the best parent in the world, or the best spouse. Whatever you do, you must apply the energy of the mind to a specific task or its wondrous powers will play mischief. There is no demon more pervasive than your own mind. So get to work.

There is another message in this story. The demon is raw, powerful energy, but it needs a power over it. The story clearly indicates that the demon, the mind, has power over matter, but it also shows that the mind needs direction. That direction does not come from the mind. Mind cannot lead mind – this direction comes from the spiritual essence. When the demon is tired, he becomes meek. This reminds me of another teaching: 'An idle mind is the devil's workshop.' The message is the same.

The Zen Ox-herding teaching depicts the mind as the wild, powerful ox. This creature, the ox, is only useful when he has been tamed. So you have this magnificent ox to pull the cart (your body) around and, disciplined, it will take you wherever you choose to go. You will have to use the whip to train it to go where you will it to go.

If we look at what the masters are telling us, it reveals something about our multidimensional nature. The mind we hold in such high esteem is but a beast. We must train it in accord with our higher nature, which is spiritual. We have all the words for these things, but until we consume the words and digest them, we don't get the point. Just as we have become so dependent on computers, we rely on information attained through the mind as if the mind itself is the central being, our core nature. The beast is strong. In reality our fundamental nature is Spirit, about which little can be said, except in metaphor.

Our practice is not so esoteric as it may appear to be on the surface. Some children are naturally inclined to do everything with their left hand. Some alert parents might guide the child to develop right-handed skills by keeping watch and correcting them. The child has both a left and a right hand anyway.

In a similar way, we are brought up in a world focusing right in on our mind and body. For many people, spirit is an afterthought. Even those who think of the spiritual make an error because they approach it through their thought-processes. They are separate from the actual experience. When your ever-present spiritual nature penetrates your consciousness, your mind takes the secondary position: you can mount this tamed ox and ride. Otherwise, sad to say, and all too often, 'The ox is riding you.'

You will have many missions in life, and most of them will be simple to accomplish … go to the store and buy some eggs for example. As you awaken each day and enter the arena, who enters? Body and mind? What you need is a link. You must never lose your connection with the *inner-net*. The spiritual disciplines mentioned, the prayer, worship and meditation, are not in themselves just means to connect or re-connect with God. They are means to thrill your spirit, to realize it is alive and real.

The Spirit and the Mind are not the same, and they are certainly not the same as you. We are made in such a way that we can speak of our parts, of ourselves, as one whole. We can say 'my mind', or 'my spirit' or 'my body', and these are different perspectives and your activity is affected by your angle of approach. So we have to be aware that we are constantly shifting gears.

In the end there is still just one you. Bite into a lemon. Your muscles contract, but who is discerning the sourness of the lemon? You can only taste the lemon with a body.

Embrace a child or another loved one: you can only do that with a body. That should be reason enough to value your bodily presence. You taste the world and spread love through this vehicle. It works. You just have to work it.

Whatever mission you take up, believe in it and give it your best. This is the Warrior Way. Miyamoto Musashi was one of the greatest Samurai who ever lived, yet his book, *Go Ren No Sho - the Book of Five Rings*, is a classic among businessmen. They found that the way and mind of a warrior worked perfectly for businessmen also.

Accept that everything you need works perfectly. Choose your direction and take the proper steps, whether it is to go to school or to open a business. Focus on that. You are not alone. You are living in a universe where every possible element that is needed to make anything work already exists. That same truth works for you. Make your steps boldly in the direction of your choice, knowing that everything and everyone you need will appear when they are needed.

There is one very important thing you must remember about this path: you must pay respect to the Master. By that I mean, we are but little spirits, fish in the Great Ocean of the Spirit. When we move with understanding, we are aware of that and pay proper respects. This is our price.

In church I remember people saying they were humbling themselves before God, but they did not appear to be doing that. However, when I began bowing in the Japanese fashion, it was out of respect to the one I could not see, but whose presence I felt. It felt wonderful because something came back. I do not bow for show or mere ritual: it is something I take pleasure in doing because I know that the marvelous and awesome experiences I have do not originate from me.

I know that, by bowing, I am opening the gate for me and the Supreme to co-mingle.

Sant Keshavadas spoke of a drop of water crying out as the wind whipped it around and the sun dried it out. The mighty ocean spoke: 'Fall into me, and I will protect you.' The drop of water was afraid he would be lost in the vastness, but he finally gave in and let go. To the surprise of the drop of water, he now shared the massive power of the ocean itself, but did not lose his individuality as water.

This is a journey of consciousness-overhaul. You enter as you, and you come out a super-charged version of you, like a favorite movie, now in 3-D. There really is no further to go. When you let go, your part of the transformation mission is already accomplished. Let the download commence.

CHAPTER NINETEEN

THE GAME

A game is for amusement, usually played in a safe place. Ideally, it should be fun. The only danger in a game played at a console, if not a bruised ego, is muscular fatigue and the like. We have the choice to stop and take a break. In playing the game, it is important that we never forget that it is a game. We are playing for fun.

The rules of the game are there to keep it fair and increase the excitement, so we should observe them. We should respect our competitor as a partner in the game – machine or human, there is no game without opposition of some kind. We should be willing to learn from the skills of the other. What begins in fun should end in fun. Be gracious.

Our everyday life is also a game. There are many players and many types of games. Some are like poker, where we must bluff, and some are like chess, where we must have strategy to succeed. In all of the games of life we use the resources given us – body, mind and spirit – to greater or lesser degrees. One thing is certain in the game of life. We need to interact with others to move on to the higher levels. There are times to play aggressively and there are times to yield and exercise humility. This chapter explores the gentler side of the game of life.

Generally speaking, we play a game to win, but just winning is meaningless without some degree of struggle, overcoming. It is therefore necessary to have a worthy opponent who can put our skill and understanding to the test. The very idea that there is someone who will challenge us with every intention of defeating us can be thrilling as well as chilling. In such a scenario we must actually produce results. Our words and all the hype before the contest do not matter.

The reason sports fans cheer so hard when their team scores a victory is that they know nothing is given. They must fight for every point. Even though the team cannot hear people yelling and screaming at their television sets, the fans give the team energy back. A great opposing team creates a great champion.

People also scream and yell for the underdog. They do this when that person shows some spark, the spirit of a champion. The Rocky movies glorified the theme of the boxing bum, whose heart and dedication alone take him to the championship. In real life, African American boxer Joe Louis faced perhaps the biggest fight of his life when he fought the poster child of the 'master race', Max Schmelling. Louis was defeated in the first match, ending his perfect record. However, he more than redeemed himself when, at the height of Hitler's propaganda campaign, he defeated Schmelling while a record 70 million people listened on the radio. In this instance Joe Louis was fighting for America, all by himself. This was one match that was not just sport.

The fact that people speak of sports figures as heroes

reveals that we are able to imbue the actions of another with a higher purpose than what they are actually doing. If a policeman or war hero gave autographs in the same mall as a football star, there would be no contest – the football star has a kind of celestial halo. His fame has a glow about it.

When a person practices something until it becomes a natural part of them, when they perform it with all they have to give, they become charismatic. Michael Jordan, the basketball star, showed this. Soccer great David Beckham has this quality and we saw that in Pelé as well. Some people are so good at what they do that they are known by people who do not follow their sport. Tiger Woods garnered movie star fame by swinging a golf club better than anyone else at the time.

There are those who play a game or sport and there are those who *live* it. When you live what you do it becomes a way of life. What you do takes on a spiritual nature far beyond the given sport or game. Miyamoto Musashi was known as *Ki sensei,* sword saint, for his mastery of the sword. An athlete comes to achieve 'sainthood' by using his skills to the fullest.

We see this recognition in the path of Yoga. It is taught that enlightenment or awakening come to be achieved through various paths – Hatha Yoga is physically based. However, the operative word is *Yoga*, which means 'union with God'. The serious practitioner is practicing to harmonize with God through a body-centered practice. The physical practice could be any activity performed with a proper attitude of mind: thus, if you practice ballet or martial arts for that purpose, they would be your Yoga. You would be taking your discipline along a higher road.

Games have rules and restrictions. Having rules and restrictions forces us to be creative while remaining conscious. Zen activity comes from the unconscious but games demand that you stay within a fixed guideline of performance. If you are unconscious you will not care about the rules – you will simply do the job.

It is for that reason that we are not likely to see true Zen at work in sports. We may see extraordinary performances and presence of mind, but Zen is not something for a game. The game is performed in a controlled environment and has a conscious beginning and ending. You must be mindful, not in No-Mind. In a game or sport you get to exercise your conscious connection with the world around you and with others also. This, too, has a purpose.

Martial art is that art which has grown out of the Way of the Warrior. Real warriors learn how to kill for real. For most people, a martial art is approached as sport. In order for them to master it they need someone to practice with and to practice on. That person, *uke* in Japanese, helps them by attempting to break through their defenses. The better the *uke*, the better the martial artist will become. Without a serious *uke*, the martial artist will get a false sense of his ability. If he or she ever need to use their skill, they need to know how it works. Like any sport, this is a conscious practice. Self-defense calls for a different attitude.

A game or sport allows you to master and practice your skills in a safe environment. Even though you face an opposing field, there is no real danger other than the occasional accident. Your attitude toward the opponent should be one of a welcoming spirit. You welcome their test of your skill. That attitude will bring forth marvelous response from you.

Now let's look at war-games for fun.

In action movies we get to experience the amazing courage and feats of the hero vicariously. Even though we know that there are special effects and CGI computer enhancements, most of us superimpose the fantasy character onto the actor. We assume that a great action or martial arts movie star is, in fact, as great as he or she may appear on the screen. That is rarely the case.

The scenes in a movie are planned down to every detail. They are choreographed. Shocking as it may be to diehard fans, even Bruce Lee staged the fights in his movies. In a video game, the images can do fantastic stunts but they are not real people and cannot be hurt. They keep coming back for more.

The Gamer/Warrior caught up in this world of fantasy may feel heroic. Within the framework of this limited world, he is a hero. There is a program, and the master player can learn to out-think or sense the sequences of the computer. There is no life and death in a war game. There is no life and death coming out of the movie screen, no matter how many gallons of fake blood spray through the air.

So action movies and war games can serve to release energy pent up from a bad day or lousy encounter. We can mentally, even spiritually, battle a foe and not get a hair misplaced or a drop of blood on our clothes. More important, there are few, if any, consequences for directing our energies into the screen or monitor, unless we fail to balance those activities with time spent in what we ironically call, the 'real world'.

Meanwhile, the real world is a misnomer: it is what we know. As they say in *The Matrix*, 'If you die here you die there.' That bit of information is an important piece of smallprint. When we step outside, there is a different scenario, a different level of the game. When we are outside of the screen or monitor, strikes, blows and cuts really hurt. Consequences exist. There is a geometric or domino effect to what happens to us or to others.

Outside we need to pay closer attention. The players of this game are three-dimensional. It is not television, it is not movies, it is not just a game. It is the most awesome X-Game of all. It is *Feel-o-Vision*. It can feel great, but it can also bring suffering and death in an instant, if you are not alert to the cues. There are cues. This is where we must step up our game. This is the high-stakes game of war where the blood is not in a bucket – it is in *you*.

Each day we hear of more tragedies. We wonder why people kill with such ease and without remorse. Yet, we have engineered that very change by creating and maintaining a fantasy industry that displays those very acts in vivid blood-like colors. Those who maim are seen delighting in their handiwork. Those who kill can smoke a cigarette afterwards or go out on the town, as if they have only shot wooden ducks in a carnival.

The problem is that something extremely important has been left out and something more important has been overlooked. We educate young ones by putting ideas in their minds. Education does not end at the school door, nor stop with the designated teacher. Young minds are constantly absorbing. Whether seated at the feet of their parents or seated before the TV, the mind takes in all that is given.

Not all people can be hypnotized. Some people exercise their minds as they read, listen or observe. These are the people who naturally screen what has entered their inner sanctum. Then there are those who are relatively defenseless. They take in this program violence as some form of intoxicating drug – they see the killing. There is nothing that suggests that it is wrong or harmful to the one pulling the trigger or stabbing the victim. How rare it is to see a character weeping over someone he has killed, or tossing and turning through a sleepless night because he is haunted by the deed.

When a child enters the fantasy world of a theater or a TV, his or her own mind becomes the holodeck which places him or her into that world. It is not so hard to get lost when there are few strong roots at home to keep that mind grounded. In the fantasy world there are absolutes – evil is truly so. We are justified to destroy the evil ones and laugh at their pain. However, outside that box things are not so absolute: the person we might think of as evil is someone's brother, father, friend, mother, daughter, wife. We may see one tiny aspect of that person in time and space while others see more.

In a world of purported law and order, our act will have dire consequences. The real danger of the fantasy view is that a person is capable of doing great harm to others, or to himself, because he does not see the dimensions of himself. He is not aware of the real person behind the eyes. He plays in a drama without the realization that there is something real going on.

Here is a test. Drop a hammer on your naked foot. How was that? I know you did not really do that and I know why: if you drop a hammer on your foot, either on purpose or unintentionally, you know what happens. Suppose you witness a hammer falling on another person's foot. If you are aligned with Original Mind, that mind in all of us, you will without hesitation hug the person to your bosom in sympathy, even if they are a stranger. They hurt, you hurt, we hurt.

The real world is not in the seeing but in the essence of those experiencing it. We see *stuff* – the universe is stuff, the Earth is stuff. Our bodies are stuff, but *we* are not stuff. The fantasy world exists in the movies, on television, in books and on stage. We are all on stage participating in what Sant Keshavadas called the *lila*, the play of the gods.

You are in a costume. You see it in the mirror. The costume is not *you*, but there is an interesting phenomenon going on. You feel everything through the costume. This interactive program is the game at the highest level. We are on the one hand an immortal soul, and on the other we are locked into mortal form capable of great suffering. Now what do we do?

What makes all of this so interesting is that even those who realize this truth as a personal experience are still subject to cause and effect. They eat, sleep, defecate and procreate just like everyone else. The real world is not what we see. It is what we *are*. In the highest sense, humankind is a fellowship of souls. When we experience our own experience, we also feel the presence of other experiences around us. People are no longer just skin-deep.

It is this realization that drives the awakened one to intervene and protect humanity. One becomes aware that there is a mistake, an error in understanding, that affects all of us ... and it does. We are so connected that, if one knocks down one person, all of us will fall in time ... and time is but an illusion of the mind.

So 'Mr Chin drinks wine and Mr Wong gets tipsy' – or is it the other way around? Well, you get the point. Millions of people love to watch the world-famous comedy basketball team, the Harlem Globetrotters, play ball. They make fools of the opposing team while playing an extraordinary game. Most people don't know that the team they play against, their *uke*, the Washington Generals, travels with them. They truly practice to win, but they do not practice to be funny. The Globetrotters are able to get away with things no other team could. They break or bend the rules at will. It is because they do that, and everyone plays along, that we all have fun.

We are all experiencing this world together. We came into awareness of it from innocence, and we each use a body vulnerable to many ills. We may be part of a team of players, but our participation or success in the game or drama of life depends on our individual performance. More important, you must be *present* to play. Do not let anyone divert you from the path. Above all, no one, absolutely no one, has the authority to take you out of the game or off the stage. If you are still here, the clock has not run out.

CHAPTER TWENTY

YOU ARE THE AVATAR

All games have rules and principles, but be certain that not everyone who plays is playing by the rules. While it is not so big a thing to lose a friendly card game or a tennis match, it is far more serious to lose your money, your car, a limb, a family member or your own wellbeing or life. Nearly all such things can be avoided, blocked, redirected or otherwise defeated by something I call the X-factor.

So much is known, so much is expected. These things can be accounted for and prepared for. That is why you must learn to be the unknown factor in the situation. That doesn't just mean that others cannot know *how* you will spontaneously respond to things, but you must also be unaware of how this survival genius will manifest within yourself in that moment.

This is not only entirely possible to cultivate, but we were all born with that genius. We had it at the very beginning of our Earth adventure. We let others dull our senses. We have embraced rules which have had the effect of binding our hands and feet, and blinding our eyes. We can no longer dance to the music as our soul interprets the rhythm: we had to do a certain dance or be laughed at as a nondancer. Acquiring the power of X, the unknown, will make you formidable in any situation, whether on the job, in a negotiation or on the street facing a gun or a knife. As far-fetched as this may sound, with the right understanding and a little practice we can play the X-Game in three dimensions. You only need one avatar: that avatar is your own body.

When I first started learning the computer, I came across a chat room. I saw people writing to each other but I also saw strange things like cartoon cups, cats and other symbols. I discovered that, since everyone was invisible to each other, these symbols represented the people who were writing. The cup could have been Sue and the cat Bobby. After awhile the cup *was* Sue. We were all invisible. We had no clue who was on the other end of the computer.

At the same time I was aware that *I am*: I am real and that realness does not depend on validation from anyone. This whole universe is a computer generated image (CGI) and your body is your avatar. Outside of the avatar there is no trace of a you to be found by the rest of us. Philosophers like to wrestle with that but, trust me, just forget it and focus on using the avatar.

In spiritual language an avatar is an incarnation of God. Let's just say we are incarnating spirits – since that is the truth for all of us, no one should feel left out or afraid. Here is where your input comes in: if you accept this designation, you must pay homage to that truth wherever you go and whatever you do. Recognizing yourself as a lower-case avatar instead of 180 pounds or more of meat, established that you are 'in this world but not of it', as Jesus said, that admittance alone puts you on a different plane. Your education will come from that higher plane.

A radio can pick up many frequencies but a satellite radio can receive far more signals. When you relax into the avatar mode you naturally ascend to a higher frequency. You come in contact with real people who would not otherwise ever cross your field. This is true because even in this world there are many dimensions functioning simultaneously, overlapping without our knowledge.

The scripture talks about Jesus, an avatar, walking through the crowd and not being seen. I am sure he was visible to himself, but he moved on a frequency that ordinary men could not pick up. By settling into this view of self and simply living from there, lessons will come. Thus, the saying, 'When the student is ready, the master will appear.' The master is not looking for a pile of meat, but he rejoices in the presence of a quickened spirit. This is made clear in the scriptures: 'God is Spirit. He seeks such as they to worship him.' It takes one to know one.

The avatar identifies his life with the Unborn, not with the linear world. Yet that same person can enjoy being present here, in this linear world. Being in the world, we can enjoy the food, go to the theater and, yes, we can even go to Disneyland. No one enjoys the Earth better than a child. The return of the childlike mind is the key to the Kingdom of Heaven.

The avatar silently appreciates his origin, which is not of this world, but the Buddha-like smile on his or her face gives a hint of the illuminating power at work within. An avatar washes dishes, sweeps floors and loves without design, by virtue of that inward power. The avatar is what the world can see, and the world needs to see something. We need you to stay here as long as you can. We need you to give us your hand, avatar. You are truly *needed*. But you must embrace X, the unknown.

The promise of this book is that you can respond like a Zen Warrior in thirty days or less. I have introduced no weapons or martial techniques, so you may naturally wonder how this transformation can be achieved. I assure you, whether you are a fit athlete or an overweight couch potato, your ability to have this experience is the same because there is but one weapon, the Mind, and none other. All else are just projections of fear. *I have no miracles; I make the Dharma my miracle.*

There was a time when my life was plagued by bullies. I spent those early years reading books, going to church and school and being quiet. I did not know why people wanted to fight me, but I was always being singled out by someone after school. I was small for my age and people naturally expected the taller, stronger boy to win. It seemed like some law: it was voiced, 'You can't do anything with him, he's too big.' It seemed to be my destiny to face foes, to come home battered and bruised.

Then something happened that pressed deeply on my mind and heart – the stabbing of Kitty Genovese, a housewife from Queens, New York. The young woman was stabbed 27 times as neighbors looked on or heard the screams. I was only nine years old, but I felt great sorrow that this woman had no one to come to help her in her hour of greatest need. My spiritual life was already strong and I believed in biblical teachings. I prayed to God to teach me how to fight, to make me strong enough to protect the weak. I wanted never to ignore a cry for help. That was a contract made in silence between God and me.

Not long after that prayer I met the Jujitsu master, then known as Sergeant C O Neal. He was a small man, but he tossed big policemen around in front of my eyes. He did this just to show me what Jujitsu was. He was still wearing his police uniform. By demonstrating his skill, Master Neal imparted a great truth, that size was not the deciding factor in combat. I was inspired.

My father added to that revelation by telling me of the conquests of Napoleon, who was also short. Now I understood that my short stature was not a barrier. Seeing Jujitsu, I became interested in learning more about the spirit behind it. By the age of twelve, I went to the library and checked out every book I could find. In that way, I discovered the Samurai and eventually the Bushido Code they lived by. I was excited.

During the time I was growing up, a black man in America was powerless to protect his family or assert his rights. Even though he may have had military background, racism and hatred were so deeply rooted in the culture that, in the deep South, killing black people was a sort of sport. This concerned me. As I drank in tales of warriors, I knew that I would never walk away from a cry for help, but neither would I allow myself to be a victim to anyone. Then my father taught me, 'Death before dishonor.' These words of Mencius rang through my soul. I did not know it then, but I had embraced 'X'. I was bowing to the East. I opened my mind and spirit to the unknown. The Asiatic spirit had merged with my own.

At first I was a victim, afraid of the fists and the feet of those who taunted me. I decided I would not allow this to happen anymore. I knew no techniques – I just had a new feeling about myself. One day I was talking to a girl in the school lunch room. A tall, jealous boy hit me in the head with a math book. Then he leaned against the wall and laughed. That was a big mistake, because I liked the girl. I stood up, took the book in hand and walked over to him.

'I believe this is your book,' I said. I shoved the book into his solar plexus with all my twelve-year old strength. He crumbled to the floor and I walked out. I walked but I wanted to run. I went to the library until the lunch period was over. The truth was that I was afraid of what would come next. Would he kill me? When the bell rang, I went into the hallway and there he was. I froze and he did something else. He ran. He saw me and was afraid. One bully down.

I acted with force and the adversary was broken down. *It is important to follow through.* It is important to put authority behind your actions. By choosing to stand up for my right to walk in peace and travel unharmed, I cut off an avenue of escape. Running away was not an option any more. If peace was to be established, it had to established through compromise or by force. I was not going to back down. So I adopted a code: *mo chi chu* – I must go straight through without looking back.

This was also a biblical admonition. Once you put your hands to the plow, you are not to turn back. While I did not know Karate, I was fascinated about breaking boards and such – in those days, people did not know much about Karate anyway. I was walking down the street when I saw some bad boys on the corner. I knew they would challenge me but I kept walking toward them. When I was close I saw a plank of wood laying in the grass. I picked it up.

'You gonna use that on us?' someone asked. I sat it down,

leaning it against a telephone pole. 'No, I don't need it,' I said. I dropped to one knee and smashed the plank in two. They had never seen anything like that. I suppose they saw their own bones cracking. They got out of my way.

The biggest test of my young life was when the worst bully I knew came up to fight me, as usual without a reason. He threw a punch and I blocked and hit him so hard in his stomach that he dropped to the sidewalk crying. I helped him up and left him with a message: 'People change.'

These things happened because of my own conscious decisions. My mind was being re-programmed so that I looked at myself and my options in a different way. I did not have any technical skills to speak of, but I had determination and a will to preserve my body. These early adventures in mental conditions laid the groundwork for what happened years later when I experienced satori.

I was not meditating to learn how to fight – I was meditating for my life. However, the years that I gave myself consciously to seasoning myself as a warrior or defender became electrified when my insight expanded in all directions and made my warriorhood *spiritual* instead of conscious. We enter where we can. If you want to ski down the mountain you need to go up the mountain. Gravity will bring you down.

I can tell you this. It's worth deciding right now to point your mind in this direction. I will always defend my loved ones and protect my right to be, and it will become so. A few years ago a top black belt, trained by famed martial artist Frank Dux, who was played by Jean-Claude Van Damme in the movie *Bloodsport*, came to my school. I let him spar with my black belt and he tossed him around like a rag doll.

I did not interfere. When it was over I knew that my student was intimidated by the rank of the person, a fifth-degree black belt, and the fame of his teacher. I stood on the mat and invited the *Bloodsport* prodigy to try me. In less than six seconds I was finished with him. He became one of my students for a while. I asked my black belt why he failed. 'He outranked me,' he said.

'No one outranks you. You are my student.' I worked with him privately for about two weeks, then arranged another match. This time my student, Moses McFarland, won. Rank had nothing to do with it.

You can change your mind. You can change your direction. Change it. Don't be *predictable*. Let 'X' be your factor. I have done a demonstration all over the world in which I ask a person to put their hand up and tell me when they are ready. They are supposed to block my hand. Not only do I strike over 99% of them before they know it, but also I bring my hand back before they can react.

That is one thing. The other is harder to grasp. I do the same thing in slow motion and still hit them. For whatever reason, they seem paralyzed – such is the penetrating power of your mind. Don't let your mind work for your adversary. *Stay in your court and be on your side.* If your mind is your friend, it has you covered. Just remember, you are conscious of only a little – there are vast regions of events and possibilities you are not aware of. Your mind accesses those dimensions also, so trust its functioning power. You can do that when you have trained or programmed it to be on your side.

When my daughter, LaKita, was a little girl, she asked me what I would do if Freddy Kruger, the demon from the

Nightmare on Elm Street movies, came after me. 'Freddy Kruger does not want to bother me,' I said. 'I would run him back where he came from.'

'You can't do anything with Freddy Kruger,' she said.

'Freddy Kruger can't handle the power in me – I am Vernon Kitabu Turner.' And that ended the discussion.

In a script written by a writer other than yourself, the demon always wins. If he comes into my territory, *I* write the script, and the demon doesn't stand a chance. The battle is fought in the real world with your mind. It is your Soul Sword, your Dharma Sword. It must work for you, or it is not working.

You face different situations and characters every day. One thing alone must be constant: remember your body is moving about here and there – it is just your avatar. Be steadfast and immovable of mind. Do that and you can relax and enjoy the Game of Life at all levels and in all circumstances.

For over 40 years I have demonstrated my mastery to experts and masters in many parts of the world. That mastery came without training by rote. It was the result of an overturning of my mind. That is what I am sharing with you, and what I share with all of my students. More important than any demonstration, no matter how impressive it is, is the fact that, whenever I hear a cry for help, I respond.

It was my original prayer. If that were not the case, I would be only a showman, not a true Zen Warrior. A Zen Warrior, like the Samurai, must lay down his body in service to humanity, or to the Lord, as indicated by the circumstances. You may not choose to go that far, but that is the distance.

When your mind changes, you are suddenly invincible.

But the source of that invincibility has no traces. That being said, we have words like *satori*, insight, a revelation from God. Whatever it is called, it is there for you to experience.

You have thirty days. The clock is going tick-tock. In thirty days, I expect you to be ready when the need arises. We always need some way to talk about things. If you never raise your hand in defense, the power will always be there beneath the surface. You will know that, within you, always ready is the Mighty Kong.

INDEX